Editor
Emily R. Smith, M.A. Ed.

Editorial Project Manager
Elizabeth Morris, Ph.D.

Editor-in-Chief
Sharon Coan, M.S. Ed.

Cover Artist
Larry Bauer

Art Coordinator
Denice Adorno

Imaging
Alfred Lau
James Edward Grace

Product Manager
Phil Garcia

Publishers
Rachelle Cracchiolo, M.S. Ed.
Mary Dupuy Smith, M.S. Ed.

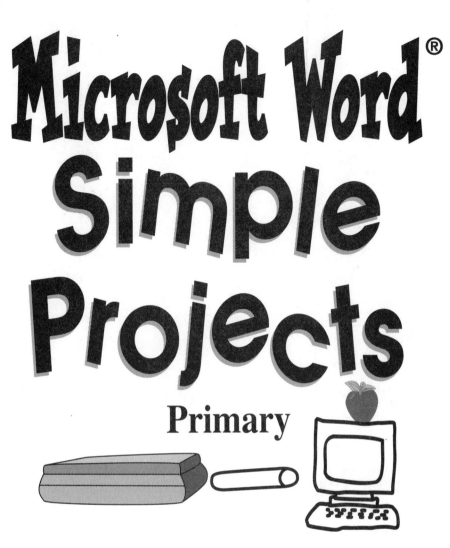

Microsoft Word®
Simple
Projects

Primary

Author

Eric LeMoine

Teacher Created Materials, Inc.
6421 Industry Way
Westminster, CA 92683
www.teachercreated.com
ISBN-1-57690-729-5

©2001 Teacher Created Materials, Inc.
Made in U.S.A.

Table of Contents

Introduction

Many teachers with one or a few computers in their classrooms have struggled with the reality of how to effectively manage equitable, authentic use of technology. In the early 1990s, when I first began using computers in my classroom, I grappled with how to incorporate the machines into my daily routine. I now realize I was missing two key ingredients in the equation.

- curriculum integration
- an effective management routine

Computer use was dominated by students who finished their work first or were receiving classroom rewards. I had various math drill software and some "educational" games the students would use. I always knew this method of computer use was not the best, but as a busy classroom teacher relatively new to technology, I did not have the time or experience to explore other methods.

After attending a few technology conferences and seeing what good technology integration looked like, I reexamined how I was using the two computers in my classroom. I realized I had not considered one very basic premise—start with my existing curriculum. As I began designing lessons for the computer centered around my curriculum, it became obvious that I needed a management system to insure equitable and orderly access for my students. Through several years of trial and error in my own classroom, and many more years working at a building level as an instructional technologist in K–5 classrooms, I refined a system that works quite well in most types of classrooms. The goal is to keep students working on authentic tasks, with a minimum of assistance on your part, while rotating through your computers as often as possible.

What follows is a detailed description of concrete ideas and tips to help you achieve this goal. As you begin to experiment with these ideas in your own teaching situation, customize and change them to fit your style and classroom needs. Include the students in your grand scheme. Be open with them and get their feedback when things are not going so well. The students can offer great insight on why a lesson on the computer went awry—either from a content or management perspective. I often found out from my students that the reason problems cropped up during the rotation was because I had not outlined expectations sufficiently, or I had not been clear enough in my directions.

Software Used for This Book

I wrote this book using *Microsoft Word 98* for the Macintosh. Hence, the screen shots, menus, etc. might look a little different if you are using a different version or platform. However, you should have no difficulty if you are using an IBM-compatible computer or a different version of *Word*. The similarities are many, and the differences are few between versions and platforms when it comes to *Microsoft Word*. To use the templates on the CD-ROM, you will need to have *Microsoft Word 97/98* or higher on either a Macintosh or Windows platform.

Curriculum Integration

Obviously (or not so obvious to me when I started using computers in my classroom!) you want the task at the computer to be tied to what you are doing in the classroom. For example, if you are a second grade teacher and your students are learning about patterns in math, you might have an activity on the computer that reinforces patterning skills you have taught. This computer activity could be in the form of math software with which the students interact (most math drill software contains patterning activities), or it could be the students creating their own patterns using the draw tools in *Microsoft Word*.

Introduction

If you don't have any software or activities that address your current teaching themes, you still have valid opportunities to provide meaningful technology experiences for your students related to your teaching. One possibility is to identify a Web site that has pictures or text information related to your classroom themes.

When your students have their turns at the computer, have a specific task for them to complete using the information from the Web site. At a very basic level, the task may be for the students to simply explore the Web site as a virtual field trip and be able to tell the class one thing they learned while visiting. Especially in the younger grades, I do not like to introduce novel material to my students using the computer. Rather, I use the computer as a way of reinforcing and extending the concepts I have already taught in the classroom.

This book has 20 different lessons that you can use as springboards to connect the computer use in your classroom to your teaching. Don't limit yourself to the activities and templates in this book! Certainly use them, but don't hesitate to alter them to fit the content you are teaching to your students. Many of the computer-related lessons I have used over the years originally came from seeing someone else's idea—I just had to change the content to fit my teaching situation.

Some Effective Management Tips

Regardless of how you schedule computer use in a classroom, there are several factors you can put into place to minimize the administration time needed to run a smooth program.

- **Give the students as much responsibility as possible for the minute-to-minute running of the computer schedule.**

   Have the students be responsible for keeping track of their time on the computer. If their time slots at the computer last 20 minutes, provide a timer of some sort that the students operate. When their time is up, they are responsible for saving and quitting the program. They are also responsible for alerting the next student(s) who is scheduled to use the station.

   When students finish at the computer and come back to the activity or lesson in the classroom, they might not know what to do. Perhaps they have missed some directions given to the class by the teacher. One of the weekly jobs I have in my classroom is the "Computer Recovery Expert." It is this student's job to quietly inform returning students what is expected of them.

   Keep a checklist of student names at the computer. When students finish their turns, they check off their names. Then, you can tell by looking at this sheet who has been to the computer and who has not.

- **Make sure that the activity you have assigned is very clear and that expectations are well understood by your students.**

   I always introduce a new computer lesson to the whole class before having students rotate through the computer station. This is easy to do if you have the ability to display your computer on a TV screen or a projector. If your building doesn't have the equipment to do this, you can buy the device to display on a TV screen for around $150. Most computer catalogs carry these devices, generically called scan converters.

Introduction

Be very precise when introducing a new lesson. Address the roles the student pairs will have at the computer. Will one have control of the mouse until it is passed to the partner? Or will a certain portion of the activity on the computer be finished by one of the students before his or her partner gets the mouse? Most students will not automatically be able to function amiably and responsibly at the computer. It will require plenty of modeling and reteaching on your part!

Depending on the grade level, I might post a list of directions at the computer that applies to the week's computer activity. I always make sure to take a moment after writing the directions to complete the activity myself, following what I have just written. I also encourage the students to give me any feedback on how to make the instructions more clear. Students who come up with good ideas are eager to update the instructions for you! Allowing the students to become an integral part of the process helps them focus on the task and can reduce management problems.

- **Have processes in place for when students need help while on the computer. They should never come to you first!**

Another job I have in my classroom is our "Computer Experts." I usually have two students in this weekly role. The job of a Computer Expert is to be the first line of defense if students at the computer(s) have a problem they cannot solve. Obviously, some students in your class will be more computer savvy than others, and students will naturally gravitate to them for help. However, it is very important that all students are given equal opportunities for the job of Computer Expert. Be up front with your kids. I tell them something like this: "Boys and girls, we know that John and Sarah know a lot about computers. But would it be fair to them if we always went to them for help? Would it be fair to the rest of us? Even if you don't know much about computers yet, do you think you could learn something by having the job of Computer Expert?"

If the students are having a problem at the computer they cannot solve, one of them quietly gets up and gets both Computer Experts. The Computer Experts return to the computer with the student. The problem is explained, and the Computer Experts attempt to solve the problem, but are not allowed to touch the mouse or any other part of the computer! If the problem cannot be solved in a reasonable amount of time (I usually set a limit of three minutes), then the student can quietly get one more student of his/her choice from the classroom to help (probably John or Sarah!). If the problem still cannot be solved, then the teacher can be approached. I work with my students to train them to know when it is okay to enlist me with computer help. There are times when I am not available (maybe I am doing a reading running record with a student), and the computer activity is then suspended until I have time to address the problem. I like to make time once or twice a week to allow the class to talk about any problems that were encountered at the computer and the solutions that were found. This helps create a common knowledge base in the classroom to assist with future problems.

This type of scenario requires a lot of modeling by the teacher and students, and it will not run smoothly the first time (or the second, or third . . .). Make sure to stop the process if it is not working and to address the problems that are occurring. Get ideas and possible solutions from your students. They can offer valuable insight into why a certain process is not working the way you had hoped.

Introduction

Scheduling Computer Time

In a very general sense, there are two methods of scheduling computer usage in a classroom. You can have a schedule that does not change (or changes little) from day to day or a schedule that is flexible and changes as your classroom needs dictate. When I first began scheduling integrated computer use in my classroom, I set up a fixed-scheduling situation, in which students rotated through the two computers in my classroom based on a pre-determined schedule. I usually had the students working in pairs, with each pair of students being assigned a number.

On the weekly schedule, I had the time slots listed with the numbers of the pairs next to the time slots. I would rotate the numbers so that the same students would have different time slots on different days. This type of scheduling worked okay some of the time, but it had its drawbacks. It took time to manage the schedule. There were times throughout the week when the assigned computer time was cancelled due to teaching situations when students could not be away from whole-class instruction. Maybe we had a new concept being introduced in math or were having a writing assessment during writer's workshop. I always seemed to be spending time tweaking the computer schedule to make sure students were getting equal time. In my experience, it is a rare classroom that has a predictable enough schedule day after day to support this type of computer scheduling without lots of time invested by the teacher. So what is the alternative?

I eventually moved to a more flexible scheduling situation. Its primary focus was to fit nicely into the current teaching day. By default, then, the schedule was different each day. This sounds like a nightmare, I know, but read on and I think you will agree it is quite easy to schedule!

In the morning, when I first got to my classroom, I would take a quick look at my lesson plan schedule for the day (you know, that little book where we have all of our lesson plans mapped out in exacting detail . . .). I identified time blocks during the day when students could afford to be away from whole-group instruction. I looked for blocks that were at least 20 minutes long. If you think about it, every schedule has some of these time blocks already built-in. What about silent reading time? It's okay for a student to miss silent reading once a week. What about a writer's workshop time? Since writing time is often a work time that is continued from one day to the next, it is a time students can miss as long as you are not introducing a new concept. If you have any project time in your schedule, this is a time that can also be used for students to be at the computer. After identifying these times, I wrote them on the board. As students came into the room, it was part of their daily routine to check the computer times (along with hanging up their coats, doing their lunch count, handing in homework, etc.).

Now the students know which time blocks are identified by you as appropriate computer times. But how do they know when it is their turn? I keep a checklist of student names at the computer. As students finish their turns at the computer, they put checks by their names. The next turn belongs to the next student on the list. If you are using partners, you would need to have partners listed next to each other on the list.

You will undoubtedly make changes and alter what I have described here to fit your needs and teaching style. One example might be the need to quickly determine who has been to the computer since a new activity was introduced. You could keep a piece of poster board hanging by the computer with a line down the middle. On one side it could say "Been to the computer," and on the other side "Have not been to computer." Students have clothespins with their names on them. As students finish their scheduled computer times during the week, they move their clothespins to the "Been to the computer" side of the poster board. You now have a quick visual way to determine how many of your students have been to the computer since you began the activity rotation.

Using This Book

Microsoft Word, as is the case with all "word processors" on the market today, is not merely a word processor. It has the capabilities of the most powerful desktop publishing programs of just a few years ago. Today's *Word* can import graphics, sounds, graphs, and movies. It can contain columns, free-floating text boxes, and three-dimensional and shadowed objects and tables. You can draw and color a limitless variety of objects. It has a spell check, thesaurus, and grammar check. The list goes on. Your primary students will certainly not be using all of the power of *Microsoft Word,* but introducing them to this software in the context of your classroom studies will give them a head start with this industry-standard program.

The lessons in this book are divided into four subject areas—language arts, science, mathematics, and social studies. Each of the subject areas has several lessons. All the lessons have an accompanying template on the CD-ROM as well as completed examples. Any time you see a planning sheet in this book for the lesson, it is also included on the CD-ROM so that you can print it out and use it with your students. Some of the lessons require the students to print out after finishing on the computer and to complete the activity at their desks by drawing or illustrating with crayons, colored pencils, or markers.

Don't limit yourself to the lessons in this book. Feel free to change the lessons and templates to better fit your teaching style and situation. As you look at the lessons and templates, you will probably get other ideas on how to use technology with your students. Specific techniques and management ideas for using and scheduling the lessons in this book can be found in the Introduction (pages 3–6).

As you explore and use these lessons with your students, directions are given on how to use the tools incorporated in each lesson. For a more complete treatise on using *Microsoft Word,* see the book *Microsoft Word for Terrified Teachers* by Paula Patton and Karla Neeley Hase (published by Teacher Created Materials).

Word Toolbars

Microsoft Word contains many toolbars, but we will be using two of them more often than the others—the formatting toolbar and the drawing toolbar. These two toolbars are discussed below with their various components.

The Formatting Toolbar

The icons from left to right on the formatting toolbar are: Style, Font, Font Size, Bold, Italic, Underline, Align Left, Center, Align Right, Justify, Numbering, Bullet, Decrease Indent, Increase Indent, Outside Border, Highlight, and Font Color.

The Drawing Toolbar

The icons from left to right on the drawing toolbar are: Draw, Select Objects, Free Rotate, AutoShapes, Line, Arrow, Rectangle, Oval, Text Box, Insert WordArt, Fill Color, Line Color, Font Color, Line Style, Dash Style, Arrow Style, Shadow, and 3-D.

Using This Book

Word Toolbars *(cont.)*

If you don't see the toolbars you want to use, you can view or hide them by pulling down the **VIEW** menu and selecting *Toolbars*. There are many toolbars, probably more than most elementary students would ever use!

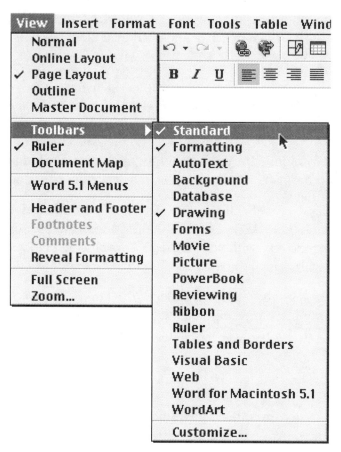

Large Screen Projecting

Before allowing your students to work on any of the lessons, familiarize yourself with the lesson and template. Conduct a whole-group lesson using a projection device, if one is available to you. The least expensive way to "project" your computer screen so the entire class can see it is to use a TV. The devices that allow you this functionality are quite common in elementary schools, so check with the technology or media person in your building—you might already have access to one! If your building does not have one, they start at about $150. If you are buying one, make sure it is compatible with your make and model of computer and TV.

Other, but more expensive (and higher resolution!) alternatives for projecting your computer screen to your class exist. LCD (liquid crystal display) panels can be bought for under $1,000, but make sure you have an overhead projector that is compatible with the panel. The most expensive (and of course, the nicest) alternative is the computer projector. The best projectors can be used with the lights on in the room (using an LCD panel requires all lights to be off) and offer superior resolution. Obviously, you can also gather your students around a computer monitor to demonstrate a lesson, but having a larger monitor than most computers have (at least 17 inches) and a small class helps out here.

Using This Book

About the CD-ROM

The CD-ROM included with this book contains the templates, planning sheets, and examples that go with the lessons. They will work on IBM-compatible (PC) or Macintosh platforms. How you choose to organize and make the templates available to your students is up to you, but two recommendations are described below.

You might want to copy all of the templates to a folder or directory on your hard drive, or you can copy them one at a time as you need them. If you ever lose the templates on your hard drive (accidental deletion, saved over, etc.), you can always get fresh copies from the CD-ROM. The easiest way to make the templates accessible for your students is to place them on your desktop. This way, the students just need to double-click on them to start an activity.

When students open templates, they need to save them under different names before changing anything, as this will preserve the templates for the next student. Make sure to train your students to pull down the **FILE** menu and select *Save As* to give each template a different name. You will want to advise them on how to name their files so that they are easily accessible at a later date.

There is a foolproof way, however, to insure that the template files you have copied to your hard drive never get accidentally saved over by a student. You can change the file into a *Microsoft Word* template file and store it in the templates folder in the *Microsoft Office* folder. To do this, follow these steps:

1. Open the Templates folder in the *Microsoft Office* folder on your hard drive. On the PC, the directory path is My Computer—C drive—Program Files—*Microsoft Office*—Templates.

2. Create a new folder in the Templates folder. You can name it something like "Simple Projects."

3. Copy the templates from the CD-ROM into this folder.

All of your templates are now stored in the Templates folder of *Microsoft Office*. To direct students to the templates, have them first launch *Microsoft Word*, and then pull down the **FILE** menu and select *New*. In the resulting dialog box, they would click on the **Simple Projects** tab at the top of the window, and then choose the correct template. The big advantage to this method is that the template is automatically opened up with the name *Document 1* and the student cannot accidentally save over the original!

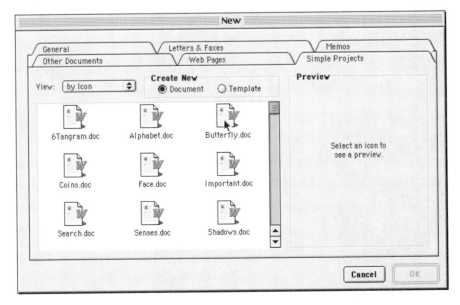

CD-ROM Filenames

Page	Activity	Template Filename	Example Filename	Planning Sheet Filename
15	Tomorrow's Alphabet	Alphabet.doc	Alphaex.doc	Alphapl.doc
19	What's in a Face?	Face.doc	Faceex.doc	
23	Plot That Web!	Web.doc	Webex.doc	Webpl.doc
29	Synonyms/Antonyms	Synant.doc	Synantex.doc	
33	WordArt Acrostic Name Poems	WordArt.doc	WrdArtex.doc	WrdArtpl.doc
38	Get Your Worms in Order!	Worm.doc	Wormex.doc	
40	The Butterfly or the Egg?	Buterfly.doc	Btrflyex.doc	
43	Animal Research	Animal.doc	Animalex.doc	Animalpl.doc
48	Shadows All Around Us	Shadow.doc	Shadowex.doc	Shadowpl.doc
54	My Five Senses Poem	Sense.doc	Senseex.doc	Sensepl.doc
58	Tangram Fun	Tangram.doc	Tangrmex.doc	
62	Six Tangram Squares	6Tangram.doc	6Tngrmex.doc	
66	Tic-Tac-Toe	Tictac.doc	Tictacex.doc	
70	Coins All aRound Us	Coin.doc	Coinex.doc	
74	Shapes, Colors, and Lines	Shape.doc	Shapeex.doc	Shape.doc
78	How Could We Get There?	There.doc	Thereex.doc	
82	The Important Thing About School	Thing.doc	Thingex.doc	Thingpl.doc
85	State Trading Cards	State.doc	Stateex.doc	Statepl.doc
89	Create your own *Word* Search	Search.doc	Searchex.doc	Search.doc

Create Your Own Clip Art Libraries

A Teacher Task

Are you ever frustrated by the lack of good thematic-related clip art in *Microsoft Word*? Don't despair! You and your students can create your own libraries of clip art in *Word*. In this exercise, we will learn how to add our own clip art to the **Microsoft Clip Gallery**. Depending on the technology comfort of your students, they could create the custom classroom libraries, or you could create them for student use. As you begin to accumulate thematic-related clip art and photographs for you and your students to use, you can build on these collections from year to year, and soon you will have a very useful assortment customized for your curriculum!

Grade Levels: 1–3

Materials:

- collections of clip art (from Web sites, digital camera pictures, scanned student artwork, etc.) related to any area of your curriculum

Before the computer:

- Brainstorm with the students the different types of pictures/clip art objects you should include in your custom clip gallery. Choose a topic to go along with a theme or unit you are teaching in your classroom.
- Decide with the students where they can get these pictures. Talk to them about possible sources—pictures that are already on the computer (perhaps from a Web site) or pictures/objects that are not (drawings, physical objects around the school or home).
- Use a digital camera or scanner to digitize those objects that are not already on the computer. Save them as JPEG or GIF files. If you are using Windows software, you can also save them as BMP files.
- Don't ignore the obvious sources—your bulletin boards (i.e., include a digital picture of a unit bulletin board in a computer project), pictures from textbooks, photos of student artwork, and scanned book covers from literature studies. You can get graphics of almost any book cover from **http://www.amazon.com**.

On the computer:

- Open a new word processing document.
- Access the **Microsoft Clip Gallery** by clicking on the **INSERT** menu and pulling down to *Picture–From File*.
- From this dialog box, click on **Import Clip**.
- Make sure to create meaningful categories that will make sense to the students. You can also add keywords for searching purposes.

Extensions:

- Allow students to use a program with paint capabilities such as *Kid Pix, HyperStudio,* or *Microsoft Paint* (comes with Windows 95 and 98) to create their own clip art. Make sure to save the drawings in a graphic format that is readable in *Word* (JPEG, GIF, or BMP are good choices).

Create Your Own Clip Art Libraries *(cont.)*

Step-by-Step Instructions

Step 1

Open a new word processing document. Pull down the **FILE** menu, choose *New*, and select **Blank Document**.

Step 2

Pull down the **INSERT** menu and choose *Picture–Clip Art*. This will bring up the **Microsoft Clip Gallery**.

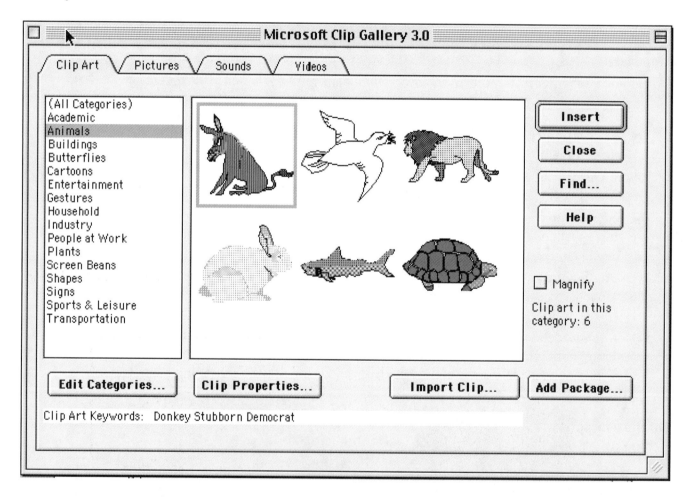

Step 3

Now click on **Edit Categories** in the **Microsoft Clip Gallery**.

Create Your Own Clip Art Libraries *(cont.)*

Step 4

You will be presented with the **Edit Category List** dialog box. Click on **New Category**, type in a name for the category of pictures you are creating, and then click on **OK** and **Close**.

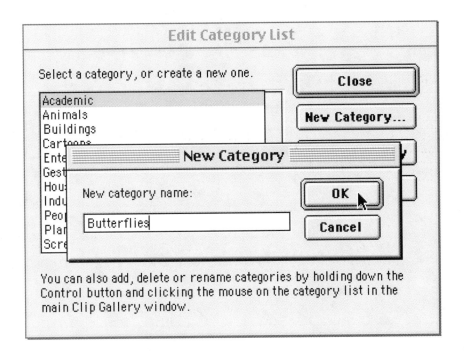

Step 5

Now you are ready to import your clip art into your newly created category. Click on **Import Clip** and locate the first picture you wish to include in your clip art category.

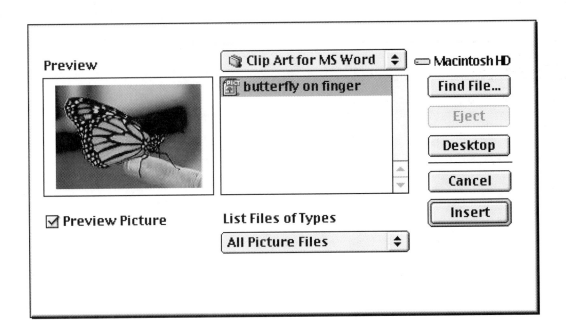

Create Your Own Clip Art Libraries *(cont.)*

Step 6

Click once on the name of the file and then click on **Insert**.

Step 7

In the resulting **Clip Properties** dialog box, make sure the correct category is checked, and then click on **OK**. You can now see your own clip art in the **Microsoft Clip Gallery**!

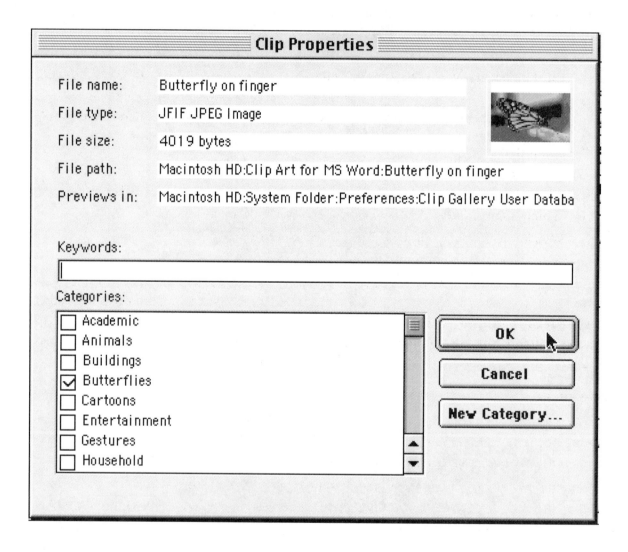

Tomorrow's Alphabet

Any study of letters and sounds should include the book *Tomorrow's Alphabet* by George Shannon. In this project, the students will create their own *Tomorrow's Alphabet* class book.

Grade Levels: K–3

Materials:

- a traditional alphabet book such as *ABC* by Jan Pienkowski or *The Alphabet Book* by P. D. Eastman
- *Tomorrow's Alphabet* by George Shannon. Another good alphabet book along the same lines is *Q Is for Duck: An Alphabet Guessing Game* by Mary Elting, et al.
- (*Alphabet.doc*) template from the CD-ROM
- copies of the **Tomorrow's Alphabet** planning sheet–page 18 (on the CD-ROM as *Alphapl.doc*)
- Internet resources: This is a Web site with published student work using the *Tomorrow's Alphabet* idea: **http://www.beavton.k12.or.us/Greenway/leahy/98-99/tomorrow/tomorrow.htm**

Before the computer:

- Read a traditional alphabet book to your students before reading *Tomorrow's Alphabet* by George Shannon. After reading both books, elicit discussion with your students with questions such as:
  - "Which book did you like best? Why?"
  - "Which one do you think would be hardest to write? Why?"
  - "Which book do you think was the most fun to write? Why?"
- Assign each student in the class a letter of the alphabet. As a whole class, have students come up with ideas for several letters to get them started (i.e., B is for flour . . . tomorrow's bread).
- Have the students fill out the planning sheets to take to the computers with them. They should illustrate their words on the planning sheets as rough drafts. They will complete their final copy illustrations after they print out their completed templates.

On the computer:

- Open the (*Alphabet.doc*) template from the CD-ROM.
- Delete the red text (*Type your name here*) and type in your name.
- Delete the red text (*Type your letter here*) and type in your letter.
- Delete the red text (*type your word here*) and type in your first word.
- Delete the red text (*type the word that begins with your letter here*) and type in your word.
- Delete the text in the boxes so that you will be able to illustrate your words after you print.

Extensions:

- Have the students make flashcards of their *Tomorrow's Alphabet* sayings with the answers on the back. They could then use them for a guessing game with their classmates.
- Cover up the words on the printouts, and see if the students can guess the sayings from the illustrations.

Tomorrow's Alphabet *(cont.)*

Step-by-Step Instructions

Step 1

Open the (*Alphabet.doc*) template from the CD-ROM.

Step 2

Make sure you have your planning sheet to look at as you work at the computer. Select the first line of red text by clicking, holding, and dragging the cursor over the text. Make sure to only select the red text.

By (Type your name here)

Step 3

Type your name to replace the red text. As long as you have selected the text, your typed text will replace the red text.

Step 4

Select the red text that says (Type your letter here).

(Type your letter here)

Step 5

Now type your letter of the alphabet to replace the red text.

Step 6

Select the red text that says (type your word here).

is for (type your word here)

Step 7

Type your first word to replace the red text.

Step 8

Select the red text at the bottom of the page that says (type the word that begins with your letter here).

(type the word that begins with your letter here).

Tomorrow's Alphabet *(cont.)*

Step 9

Type your word that begins with your letter to replace the red text.

Step 10

Select the text in the first box where you will be drawing your picture of your word after you print.

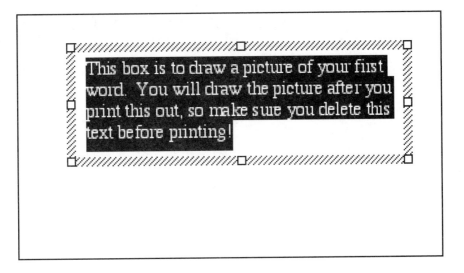

Step 11

Delete the selected text using the **Delete** or **Backspace** key on the keyboard.

Step 12

Repeat steps 10 and 11 for the second box.

Step 13

To save your document, pull down the **FILE** menu and select *Save As*. Give your file the name (*senses your initials*).

Step 14

To print, pull down the **FILE** menu and select *Print*. Click **OK** (PC) or **Print** (Mac).

Step 15

After printing, use colored pencils, markers, or crayons to illustrate your words.

Tomorrow's Alphabet *(cont.)*

Name _____

Planning Sheet

_____ is for _____

[ ]

tomorrow's

[ ]

What's in a Face?

A Drama Activity

Explore with your students the wide range of emotions the face can portray! In this project, students will look at pictures of their classmates' faces and write descriptive words or sentences to describe them. Students will gain experience inserting pictures into documents and practice keyboarding skills.

Grade Levels: 1–3

Materials:

- *Faces* by Shelly Rotner (or any book/video that depicts faces in a range of emotions)
- digital camera for photographing student faces (or regular photos and a scanner)
- chart paper on which to record brainstorming session
- (*Face.doc*) template from the CD-ROM

Before the computer:

- Read the book *Faces* by Shelly Rotner (or any book that depicts faces in a range of emotions). Before reading the book, ask students to make predictions about the story.
- After reading the book, brainstorm with the students a list of emotions/feelings that people can show with their faces. Narrow the list to a reasonable number (6–10).
- As a group, have the students make faces to illustrate the feelings from the list.
- Allow each student to choose a feeling and photograph his/her face while he/she acts out the feeling. Make sure each feeling from the list is represented.
- The digital photographs can all be stored in the same folder on your hard drive. A better option might be to import them into a custom clip art gallery (see pages 11–14). Make sure to name the pictures using the feeling/emotion depicted.

On the computer:

- Open the (*Face.doc*) template from the CD-ROM.
- Using either the **INSERT–*Picture*** or **INSERT–*Clip Art*** menu (if a custom clip art gallery was created), insert a picture of a face into your document.
- Resize the picture so it fits into the banner, and drag it to the center.
- Type a word, phrase, or sentence in the text box telling about the face.

Extensions:

- Have the students place several pictures in a row, and then tell a story that corresponds to the emotions depicted by the faces.

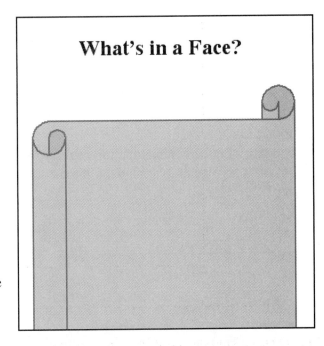

What's in a Face? *(cont.)*

Step-by-Step Instructions

Step 1

Open the (*Face.doc*) template from the CD-ROM.

Step 2

Pull down the **INSERT** menu and drag down to ***Picture***. If the pictures of the faces have been imported into a custom clip art gallery, select ***Clip Art*** and go to step 3. If the pictures of the faces have been saved to a folder, select ***From File*** and go to step 4.

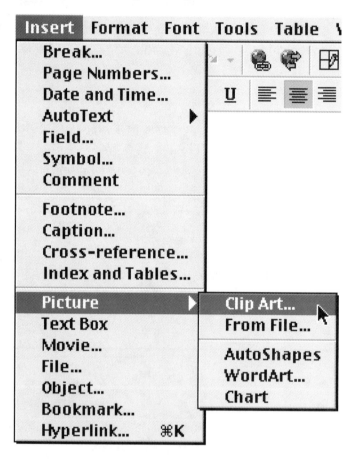

Step 3

Click on the **Pictures** tab at the top of the window, and then click on the correct category on the left. You should now be able to click on the picture of your choice and then click on **Insert**. Proceed to step 5.

What's in a Face? *(cont.)*

Step 4

You are presented with a dialog box from which you must maneuver through the directory structure of your hard drive to find the folder where you saved the pictures from the digital camera. When you find the picture, click on it once, and click on **Insert**.

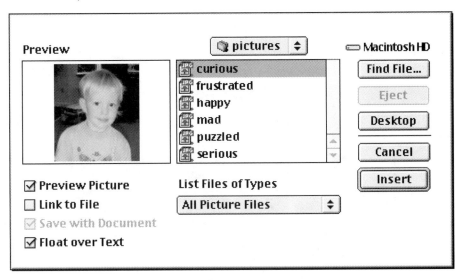

Step 5

The picture is inserted into your document. Resize the picture so it fits inside the banner. You can resize it by clicking on a corner handle and dragging diagonally.

Step 6

Let's move the picture. Click and hold on the center of the picture, and drag it to the middle of the banner. If you can't move your picture, you need to change it to a floating picture. To do this, click on your picture once to select it. Now go to the **FORMAT** menu and select *Picture*. In the dialog box, click on the **Position** tab, and then on **Float Over Text**. Click on **OK**.

Step 7

Now you are ready to type a word or sentence describing the emotion or feeling of the face. Select the text in the box below the banner by clicking, holding, and dragging across it. Then type in your word or sentence about the emotion.

Step 8

To save your document, pull down the **FILE** menu and select *Save As*. Give your file the name (*face your initials*).

Step 9

If you want to print, pull down the **FILE** menu and select *Print*. Click **OK** (PC) or **Print** (Mac).

What's in a Face? *(cont.)*

Example Page

I am very curious!!

Plot That Web!

A Story Organizer

In this project, students will create story webs based on either books they have read or a book that has been read to them. While completing the project, students will gain experience with selecting, deleting, and entering text in *Microsoft Word*.

Grade Levels: 2–3

Materials:

- books the students have read or one that has been read to them
- copies of the **Plot That Web**! planning sheet–page 26 (also available on the CD-ROM as *Webpl.doc*)
- (*Web.doc*) template from the CD-ROM

Before the computer:

- Read a short book to the class, such as *Ira Sleeps Over* or *Caps for Sale*. Make sure that the book has all of the elements needed to fill out a story web.
- Based on the book you read to the class, conduct a whole-class lesson with your students, filling out a **Plot That Web!** planning sheet together. Each child should be filling out his or her planning sheet as you do one on an overhead or butcher paper.
- Before the children go to the computer, they should have completed planning sheets. They can use the one created as a whole class or ones they created from books they have read independently.

On the computer:

- Open the (*Web.doc*) template from the CD-ROM.
- Select the red text in the *Setting* box and delete it. Now type in a sentence or two telling about the setting in your book.
- Repeat for the *Character, Problem,* and *Conclusion* boxes.

Extensions:

- Allow the students to extend the story webs by adding another category (their favorite part, what they would change in the book, etc.). The students can copy and paste one of the existing categories to make new ones. They will need to rearrange the elements on the page to make room for the additional one.

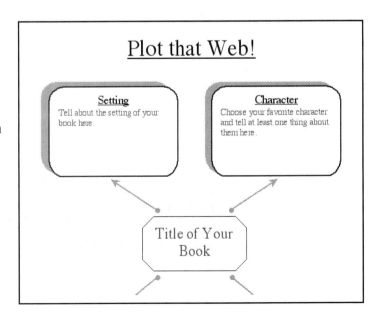

Plot That Web! *(cont.)*

Step-by-Step Instructions

Step 1

Open the (*Web.doc*) template from the CD-ROM.

Step 2

Start with the *Title* box. Select the red text in the box by clicking, holding, and dragging across the text. You will know it is highlighted because it changes color.

Step 3

Type in the title of your book.

Step 4

If the box is not big enough to hold all of your text, you can make it bigger. Move the mouse to the corner of the box over one of the selection handles. The cursor will change into a double arrow.

Step 5

Now click, hold, and drag the mouse to make the box bigger.

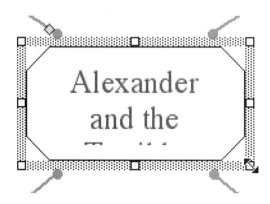

Plot That Web! *(cont.)*

Step 6

Now let's do the *Setting* box. As you did with the *Title* box, select the red text by clicking, holding, and dragging across the text. You will know it is highlighted because it changes color.

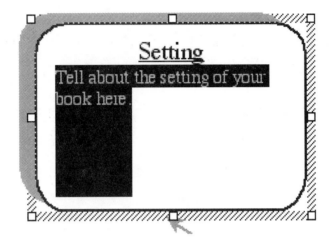

Step 7

Type in a few sentences telling about the setting of your book.

Step 8

Repeat steps 6 and 7 for the *Problem, Character,* and *Solution* boxes.

Step 9

To save your document, pull down the **FILE** menu and select *Save As*. Give your file the name (*storyweb your initials*).

Step 10

If you want to print, pull down the **FILE** menu and select *Print*. Click **OK** (PC) or **Print** (Mac).

Plot That Web! *(cont.)*

Planning Sheet

Name _____

Directions: Use this activity page to write about your book.

Title _____

Setting _____

_____

_____

Characters _____

_____

Problem _____

_____

_____

Conclusion _____

_____

Plot That Web! *(cont.)*

Template

Setting

Tell about the setting of your book here.

Character

Choose your favorite character and tell at least one thing about him or her here.

Title of Your Book

Problem

What was the problem in your book?

Conclusion

How did your book end? Was the problem solved? Tell a little about this here.

Plot That Web! *(cont.)*

Example Page

Setting

This story takes place in the country. Most of the story happens under a tree.

Character

My favorite characters were the monkeys. They were very funny with those hats on!

Caps for Sale

Problem

The problem in the book was that the monkeys took the peddler's caps. The peddler wanted them back, but the monkeys just copied everything he did.

Conclusion

Finally, the peddler took off his cap and threw it down. Then the monkeys did the same thing, and the peddler had all his caps back!

Synonyms/Antonyms

In this project, students will match antonyms and synonyms. While completing the project, they will gain experience using the line tool in *Microsoft Word*. This project is easily adaptable by the teacher or students for other types of word pairs (similes, compound words, homophones, etc.).

Grade Levels: 1–3

Materials:

- (*Synant.doc*) template from the CD-ROM
- a student-brainstormed list of antonyms and synonyms (perhaps a list that is related to a current unit of study)

Before the computer:

- Have the students make antonym and synonym flashcards from lists that are class generated. They can write one word on the front of the card and the antonym (or synonym) on the back.
- Allow the students to play games with the flashcards. Brainstorm with them what kinds of games could be played. Let them come up with game ideas and rules.
- Ask the students: "Can a word have more than one antonym or more than one synonym? Can you give me some examples?"

On the computer:

- Open the (*Synant.doc*) template from the CD-ROM.
- Use the **Line** tool to draw lines between the antonyms and synonyms.
- Can you think of additional antonym pairs, or second antonyms for any of the words? What about the synonyms? If so, add the words to the template and match them up.

Extensions:

- Show the students how to use different color lines so they stand out from each other. After creating the line, go to the **Line Color** tool on the **Drawing Toolbar** and select a color.
- Have the students create antonym and synonym template lists that are related to a unit of study. Then other students can solve the student-made templates.
- The teacher or the students could create templates for other types of word pairs—similes, compound words, homophones, etc.

Antonyms		Synonyms	
fast	white	fast	spotless
short	tall	small	little
rude	night	busy	moist
black	slow	wet	quick
day	go	enormous	huge
stop	dry	neat	skinny
hot	polite	thin	pointed

Partial image of *Synant.doc*

Synonyms/Antonyms *(cont.)*

Step-by-Step Instructions

Step 1

Open the (*Synant.doc*) template from the CD-ROM.

Step 2

Start with the list of antonyms in the left column. Make sure you have access to the **Drawing Toolbar**. Pull down the **VIEW** menu and select *Toolbars*. From the toolbar pop-up menu, move over to the right and down to *Drawing*.

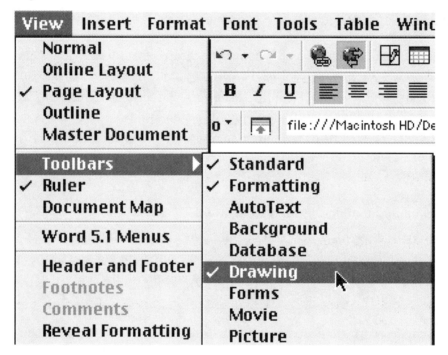

Step 3

Select the **Line** tool by clicking on it.

Step 4

Move your cursor next to one of the words on the left and click and hold the mouse. Draw a line by dragging the mouse to the antonym for that word on the right side of the column.

Synonyms/Antonyms *(cont.)*

Step 5

You can make the lines different colors by using the **Line Color** tool on the **Drawing Toolbar**.

Step 6

You can also change each line's thickness using the **Line Style** tool.

Step 7

Repeat step 4 for the rest of the words in the Antonyms column.

Step 8

Repeat step 4 for the Synonyms column.

Step 9

To save your document, pull down the **FILE** menu and select *Save As*. Give your file the name (*synant your initials*).

Step 10

If you want to print, pull down the **FILE** menu and select *Print*. Click **OK** (PC) or **Print** (Mac).

Synonyms/Antonyms *(cont.)*

Example Page

Antonyms

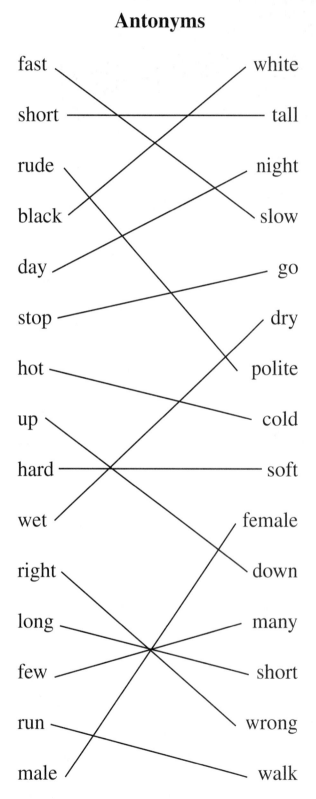

fast — white
short — tall
rude — night
black — slow
day — go
stop — dry
hot — polite
up — cold
hard — soft
wet — female
right — down
long — many
few — short
run — wrong
male — walk

Synonyms

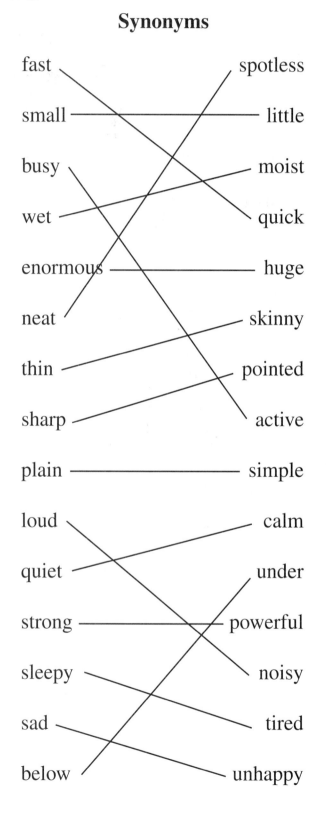

fast — spotless
small — little
busy — moist
wet — quick
enormous — huge
neat — skinny
thin — pointed
sharp — active
plain — simple
loud — calm
quiet — under
strong — powerful
sleepy — noisy
sad — tired
below — unhappy

WordArt Acrostic Name Poems

This project is a new "twist" on an old idea. The students will write an acrostic poem using their names. They will use the WordArt feature of *Microsoft Word* to give more personality and meaning to their poems than if they only used a regular font.

Grade Levels: 1–3

Materials:

- (*WordArt.doc*) template from the CD-ROM
- copies of the **WordArt Acrostic Name Poems** planning sheet–page 36 (also available on the CD-ROM as *WrdArtpl.doc*)
- a class-generated list of descriptive words for each letter of the alphabet
- a book with an acrostic emphasis, such as the series from Steven Schnur: (optional)
    - *Autumn: An Alphabet Acrostic* by Steven Schnur
    - *Spring: An Alphabet Acrostic* by Steven Schnur
    - *Summer: An Alphabet Acrostic* by Steven Schnur

Before the computer:

- Explain to the students that they will be creating poems using their names as a starting point.
- Expose the students to acrostic poems. You could introduce the concept using your school's name.
- Brainstorm with the students descriptive words for all the letters you will need for the class (Hopefully, no one has the letter "x" in his/her name!) and write them on chart paper.
- Pass out the planning sheets and model for each student how to write his/her name vertically with several possibilities for each letter of the name.
- Model for the students how to create and manipulate WordArt.

On the computer:

- Open the (*WordArt.doc*) template from the CD-ROM.
- Using the **WordArt** tool, change the text "*Yourname*" to your name.
- Use the **WordArt** tool again to create the words you have chosen for each letter of your name. Use WordArt effects that match the descriptive words you have chosen.
- Use the **WordArt** tool one last time to type your name at the bottom of the page.

Extensions:

- The acrostic poem theme can be used across the curriculum. Let your students come up with ideas on how they can use other subjects/themes for acrostic poems.
- Allow students to act out their poems. You will get some very creative actors/actresses!

WordArt Acrostic Name Poems *(cont.)*

Step-by-Step Instructions

Step 1

Open the (*WordArt.doc*) template from the CD-ROM.

Step 2

Click once on the WordArt. You have to make sure you are clicking directly on one of the letters, not in between them. When you click on the WordArt, you get the **WordArt Toolbar**.

Step 3

On the **WordArt Toolbar**, click on **Edit Text**. In the **Edit WordArt Text** dialog box, replace the text "yourname" with your name. You can also change the font, size, and style of the text from this box. Click on **OK** when you are done.

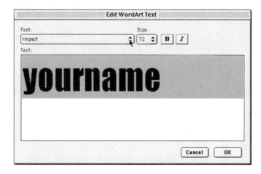

Step 4

Now you are ready to create some WordArt from scratch. We'll begin with the word that starts with the first letter of your name. From the **WordArt Toolbar** or the **Drawing Toolbar**, click on the **WordArt** tool.

Step 5

Choose a WordArt style from the **WordArt Gallery** dialog box. Don't worry, you can always change this later. Choose a style that matches the word you have picked. Click on **OK**.

Step 6

Now you get the **Edit WordArt Text** dialog box again. Type in your word. Remember, you don't need the first letter of the word, because it is already in your name!

WordArt Acrostic Name Poems *(cont.)*

Step 7

You can now see your WordArt! If you like, you can click on the **WordArt Shape** tool to change the shape of your WordArt. Just make sure your WordArt is selected before you click on the tool.

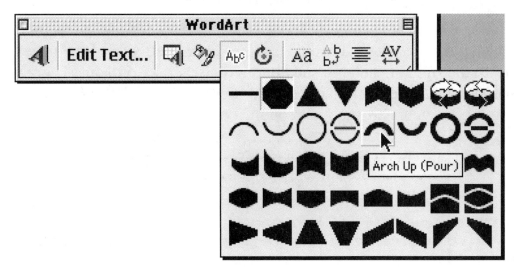

Step 8

You can use the handles surrounding your WordArt to resize and reshape it. Experiment with these to make your WordArt a size that matches your name well.

Step 9

Repeat steps 4–8 to create WordArt for the rest of your name's letters.

Step 10

Create one last WordArt at the bottom of the page with your whole first name. This will be the end of your poem.

Step 11

To save your document, pull down the **FILE** menu and select *Save As*. Give your file the name (*wordart your initials*).

Step 12

If you want to print, pull down the **FILE** menu and select *Print*. Click **OK** (PC) or **Print** (Mac).

WordArt Acrostic Name Poems *(cont.)*

Name _____

Planning Sheet

Directions: Use this sheet to brainstorm descriptive words for the letters of your name. Write your name in large letters down the squares on the left side of the page. Then use the two lines to the right of each big square to write several words that begin with that letter of your name. Circle your favorite word for each letter of your name. This will be the word you use for your acrostic poem on the computer.

WordArt Acrostic Name Poems *(cont.)*

Example Page

Directions: Use the WordArt to write words that describe you. Make sure to think of words that start with the letters of your name.

Get Your Worms in Order!

Scientific Cycles

If your students need practice selecting and dragging graphic objects in *Microsoft Word*, this activity is a fun way to do it! The students will also reinforce their knowledge of the life cycle of the mealworm.

Grade Levels: 1–2

Materials:

- mealworm colony (optional)
- (*Worm.doc*) template from the CD-ROM

Before the computer:

- Review with the students the life cycle of a mealworm. If you need some background information on mealworms, take a look at the Web sites in the resources section below.
- For younger students or students who might need extra help, print out a copy of the template. Allow the students to cut out the life cycle stages and put them in order, gluing them onto a piece of construction paper. They can then take that paper to the computer for guidance.
- Divide the class into groups of three and assign each child in the group one of the three stages. Have the students in each group arrange themselves in the order of the life cycle.

On the computer:

- Open the (*Worm.doc*) template from the CD-ROM.
- Use the mouse to click, hold, and drag on the pictures to rearrange them into the correct order of the life cycle of a mealworm.
- If desired, the students can make the pictures smaller by clicking, holding, and dragging on any corner of a picture.

Extensions:

- Allow the students to visit the Web sites listed below to learn more about mealworms.
- Set up a mealworm colony in your classroom so the students can witness the life cycle firsthand. You can refer to the Web sites to learn how to do this. It is easy to do, very low maintenance, and the student interest is very high!

Get Your Worms in Order!

Drag the three stages of the mealworm life cycle so they are in the correct order.

adult   pupa   larva

Internet Resources:

http://www.thewildones.org/Curric/mealworm.html

http://www.thewildones.org/Curric/mealLoco.html

http://www.ag.ohio-state.edu/~ohioline/hyg-fact/2000/2093.html

http://www.wayland.k12.ma.us/claypit_hill/saylor/mealworms/mealwormsonweb.html

Get Your Worms in Order! *(cont.)*

Step-by-Step Instructions

Step 1

Open the template called (*Worm.doc*) from the CD-ROM.

Step 2

If you have cut out the life cycle stages and glued them onto construction paper, make sure you have the paper with you at the computer.

Step 3

Click and hold the mouse on the pictures one at a time to drag them into the correct order.

Step 4

The pictures can also be resized to better fit on the page. To do this, click and hold on a corner of a picture, and drag it to make it bigger or smaller.

Step 5

To save your document, pull down the **FILE** menu and select *Save As*. Give your file the name (*mealworm your initials*).

Step 6

If you want to print, pull down the **FILE** menu and select *Print*. Click **OK** (PC) or **Print** (Mac).

The Butterfly or the Egg?

Scientific Cycles

This project is very similar to the previous one, except that the students will be ordering the life cycle stages of the Monarch butterfly. If your students need practice selecting and dragging graphic objects in *Microsoft Word*, this activity is a fun way to do it! The students will also use the arrow tool to draw arrows between the stages.

Grade Levels: 1–2

Materials:

- Monarch butterfly chrysalis to observe to observe life cycle firsthand (optional)
- (*Buterfly.doc*) template from the CD-ROM

Before the computer:

- Review with the students the life cycle of a Monarch butterfly. If you need some background information on Monarchs, take a look at the Web sites in the resources section below.
- For younger students, or students who might need extra help, print out a copy of the template. Allow the students to cut out the life cycle stages and put them in order, gluing them onto a piece of construction paper. They can then take the paper to the computer for guidance.
- Divide the class into groups of four and assign each child in the group one of the four stages. Have the students in each group arrange themselves in the order of the life cycle.

On the computer:

- Open the (*Buterfly.doc*) template from the CD-ROM.
- Use the mouse to click, hold, and drag on the pictures to rearrange them into the correct order of the life cycle of a Monarch butterfly.
- If desired, the students can make the pictures smaller by clicking, holding, and dragging on any corner of a picture.
- Draw arrows between the stages to make the order clear.

Extensions:

- Allow the students to visit the Web sites listed below to learn more about Monarch butterflies.
- Obtain a Monarch chrysalis so the students can witness the life cycle firsthand. You can refer to several of the Web sites to learn how to do this. It is easy to do, very low maintenance, and the student interest is very high!

Internet Resources:

> http://www.connectingstudents.com/themes/birds.htm
>
> http://www.monarchwatch.org/
>
> http://www.learner.org/jnorth/
>
> http://www.internet-at-work.com/hos_mcgrane/butterflies/index.html

The Butterfly or the Egg? *(cont.)*

Step-by-Step Instructions

Step 1

Open the template called (*Buterfly.doc*) from the CD-ROM.

Step 2

If you have cut out the life cycle stages and glued them onto construction paper, make sure you have the paper with you at the computer.

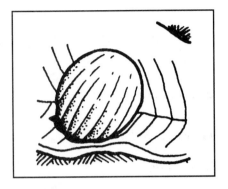

Step 3

Click and hold the mouse on the pictures and drag them into the correct order.

Step 4

The pictures can also be resized to better fit on the page. To do this, click and hold on a corner of a picture, and drag it to make it bigger or smaller.

Step 5

Click on the **Arrow** tool. Draw an arrow from the first stage to the second stage by clicking, holding, and dragging.

Step 6

Repeat step 5 to draw arrows from the second stage to the third stage and from the third stage to the fourth stage.

Step 7

To save your document, pull down the **FILE** menu and select *Save A*s. Give your file the name (*monarch your initials*).

Step 8

If you want to print, pull down the **FILE** menu and select *Print*. Click **OK** (PC) or **Print** (Mac).

The Butterfly or the Egg? *(cont.)*

Example Page

Directions: Drag the four stages of the Monarch butterfly life cycle so they are in the correct order. Once they are in order, draw arrows to show the right order.

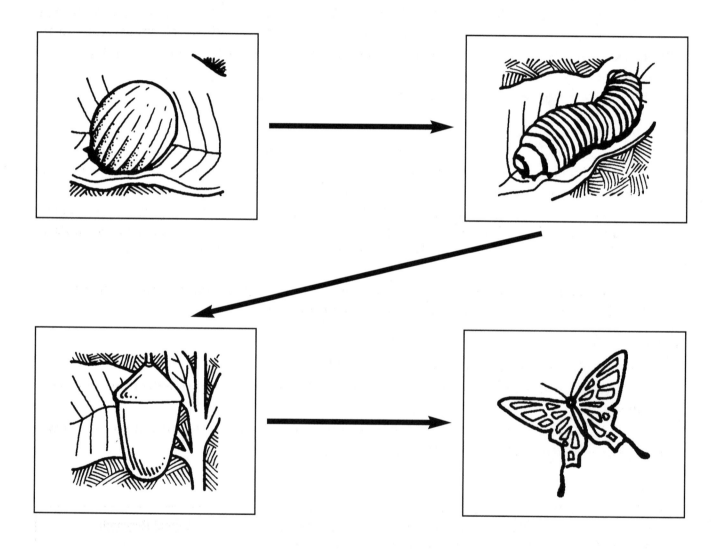

Animal Research

This project can be used as part of an existing unit on animals or as a research project by itself. Students will do basic research on animals of their choice and present their findings in a *Microsoft Word* document. Basic techniques will be used to teach researching skills to even your lowest readers!

Grade Levels: 1–3

Materials:

- many books on animals at various reading levels—include captivating picture books so your low and nonreaders can get facts from the pictures. (*The Kingfisher First Animal Encyclopedia* by Jon Kirkwood is an excellent example of a nonfiction resource text for early reader animal research.)
- copies of the **Animal Research** planning sheet–page 45 (also available on the CD-ROM as *Animalpl.doc*)
- (*Animal.doc*) template from the CD-ROM

Before the computer:

- Read aloud a short picture book having to do with animals. While you are reading, help the students with identifying facts and characteristics about the animals. Focus on text and pictures to assist the students in picking out key words and facts.
- To introduce the concept, you might want to do a whole-class lesson using the same animal and a shared resource. Have the students fill out the planning sheet with you as the class picks out facts from the resource. Make sure to allow your low and nonreaders to get information from the pictures.
- Before the children go to the computer, they should have completed planning sheets (either the one filled out as a class, or ones they filled out on their own animals).

On the computer:

- Open the (*Animal.doc*) template from the CD-ROM.
- Select the red text in the *Name of Your Animal* box and delete it. Now type in the name of your animal.
- Select the red text in the *Habitat* box. Type in where your animal lives and what life is like there.
- Repeat for the *Food, Enemies,* and *Appearance* boxes.

Extensions:

- Allow the students to extend their research by adding other categories to their papers (lifespan, number of young, etc.). The students can copy and paste one of the existing categories to make new ones. They may need to rearrange the elements on the pages to make room for the additional ones.
- The students can insert digital pictures of their animals into their reports. See the "*Microsoft Word*: Tips and Tricks" section on page 95 to see how to copy pictures from the Internet and insert them into *Microsoft Word*.

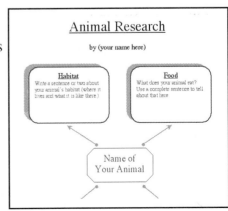

Animal Research *(cont.)*

Step-by-Step Instructions

Step 1

Open the (*Animal.doc*) template from the CD-ROM.

Step 2

Start with the *Name of Your Animal* box. Select the red text in the box by clicking, holding, and dragging across the text. You will know it is highlighted because it changes color.

Step 3

Type in the name of your animal.

Step 4

Now let's write about your animal's habitat. As you did with the name of your animal, select the red text by clicking, holding, and dragging across the text. You will know it is highlighted because it changes color.

Step 5

Type in a few sentences telling about the habitat of your animal. Don't just tell where it lives—tell a little about the environment there. Is it cold? hot? wet? dry?

Step 6

Repeat steps 4 and 5 for the *Problem, Character,* and *Solution* boxes.

Step 7

To save your document, pull down the **FILE** menu and select *Save A*s. Give your file the name (*storyweb your initials*).

Step 8

If you want to print, pull down the **FILE** menu and select *Print*. Click **OK** (PC) or **Print** (Mac).

Animal Research *(cont.)*

Name _____

Planning Sheet

Directions: Use this page to record information about your animal.

My animal is _____

My animal lives (habitat) in the _____

_____

_____

My animal eats _____

_____

Describe what your animal looks like.

_____

_____

My animal's enemies are _____

_____

Animal Research *(cont.)*

Template

Habitat

Write a sentence or two about your animal's habitat (where it lives and what it is like there).

Food

What does your animal eat? Use a complete sentence to tell about that here.

Name of Your Animal

Enemies

Use at least one sentence to tell about your animal's enemies here.

Appearance

What does your animal look like? Use some good describing words to tell about your animal.

Animal Research *(cont.)*

Example Page

Habitat

The polar bear lives in the Arctic. They do not live in the Antarctic. It is very cold in the Arctic, and they have long winters there.

Food

Polar bears eat a lot! They eat seals and fish. They have to eat a lot to stay warm.

Polar Bear

Enemies

The only real enemy of the polar bear is man. No other animals can hurt the polar bear.

Appearance

Polar bears are very big and have white fur. They have very big paws so they don't sink into the snow.

Shadows All Around Us

Science Inquiry

In this project, students will use the **Shadow** tool to indicate their understanding of where a shadow should fall based on the position of the sun.

Grade Levels: 1–3

Materials:

- one or more of the following books:
  - *Bear Shadow* by Frank Asch
  - *My Shadow* by Robert Louis Stevenson
  - *Guess Whose Shadow?* by Stephen R. Swinburne (great for explaining/investigating shadows)
  - *Nothing Sticks Like a Shadow* by Ann Tompert
- wood blocks or anything that would cast a shadow
- flashlight or direct light source for casting shadows
- globe and/or model of the earth and sun (optional)
- copies of the **Shadows All Around Us** planning sheet–page 52 (also available on the CD-ROM as *Shadowpl.doc*)
- (*Shadow.doc*) template from the CD-ROM

Before the computer:

- Read one of the books mentioned above to students or any book that addresses shadows.
- Conduct a whole-class demonstration lesson on shadow casting. This can be done in the early morning with the sun at a low angle or in a dimly lit room with a flashlight acting as the sun. If desired, you can relate the time of day/position of shadows to the daily cycle of earth rotation and of the sun hitting the earth.
- Allow the children, in small groups, to experience shadow casting on their own. The students can work from the **Shadows All Around Us** planning sheet.

On the computer:

- Open the (*Shadow.doc*) template from the CD-ROM.
- Using the **Shadow** tool, cast a shadow in the proper direction based on the position of the sun.

Extensions:

- Allow the students to move the sun on the template and adjust the shadows for the new sun position.
- Have the students create their own templates—a little differently! Instead of determining which direction a shadow would be cast by looking at the position of the sun, the student could create shadowed objects, and have a classmate determine the position of the sun.
- Pose the question—Would the shadows look the same at 10:00 in the morning on June 1st and December 1st? Why or why not?
- Would the shadows look the same in your town and in [choose a location in an opposite hemisphere at approximately the same longitude] at the same time on the same day?

Shadows All Around Us *(cont.)*

Step-by-Step Instructions

Step 1
Open the (*Shadow.doc*) template from the CD-ROM.

Step 2
Start with the first rectangular cube in the upper left corner. Note that the sun is behind the cube.

Step 3
Click once on the cube to select it. You should see the selection handles around the cube, but not around the sun.

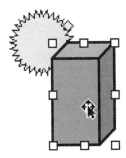

Step 4
Make sure you have access to the **Drawing Toolbar**. Pull down the **VIEW** menu and select *Toolbars*. From the toolbars pop-up menu, move over to the right and down to *Drawing*.

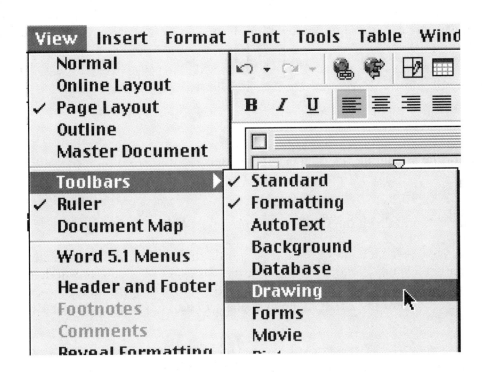

Shadows All Around Us *(cont.)*

Step 5

From the **Drawing Toolbar**, click on the **Shadow** tool, and the **Shadow Styles** will pop up.

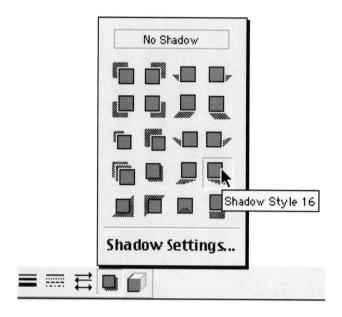

Step 6

Drag the mouse and choose the shadow style which best fits the shadow you think would be cast from the cube.

Step 7

Repeat steps 3–6 for the remaining five shapes on the page.

Step 8

To save your document, pull down the **FILE** menu and select *Save As*. Give your file the name (*shadow your initials*).

Step 9

If you want to print, pull down the **FILE** menu and select *Print*. Click **OK** (PC) or **Print** (Mac).

Shadows All Around Us *(cont.)*

Template

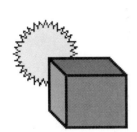

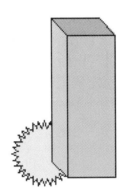

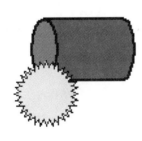

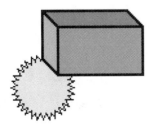

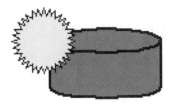

Shadows All Around Us

Shadows All Around Us *(cont.)*

Name _____

Planning Sheet

Directions: Place four objects that are at least two inches tall (small wooden blocks work nicely) on the squares on the paper. If you can't do it outside in the sun, be creative indoors. Try using a flashlight or some other point source of light. Use a pencil to shade the shadows where they are cast on the paper.

Shadows All Around Us *(cont.)*

Example Page

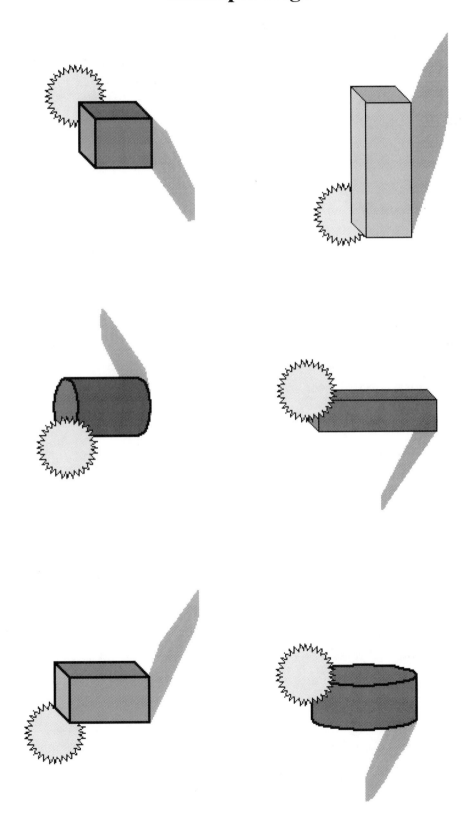

Shadows All Around Us

My Five Senses Poem

A study of the five senses is a part of many primary classrooms. Even if you don't do a unit on the senses, this is a fun and meaningful activity for your students. In this activity, the students will choose their favorite foods and write poems that include each of the five senses—touch, taste, smell, sight, and hearing.

Grade Levels: 1–3

Materials:

- a book on the five senses such as:
  - *My Five Senses* by Aliki
  - *The Five Senses* by Sally Hewitt
  - *Touch* by Maria Rius
  - *Smell* by Maria Rius
  - *Taste* by Maria Rius
  - *Hearing* by Maria Rius
  - *Sight* by Maria Rius
- (*Sense.doc*) template from the CD-ROM
- copies of the **My Five Senses Poem** planning sheet–page 57 (also available on the CD-ROM as *Sensepl.doc*)
- Internet resources:
  http://www.sedl.org/scimath/pasopartners/senses/welcome.html

Before the computer:

- Read *My Five Senses* by Aliki, or any of the other books listed above, to your students.
- Set up five stations around the room, one for each sense. Allow the students to rotate through the stations, using their senses to experience the items at each station. You may or may not choose to have the students take some notes as they do this. Examples for the stations might include:
  - Touch—sandpaper, felt, ice, an apple
  - Smell—a lemon (cut open), a flower, dirt, mentholatum
  - Taste—candy-coated chocolates, lemonade, sugar, salt (make sure you take precautions with sanitation)
  - Hearing—a cassette tape with music, a volunteer biting an apple, a computer mouse
  - Sight—duplicate some of the items from the other four senses
- Discuss the following questions with your students after they finish with the stations:
  - "At the taste station, did you use any other sense besides taste? Which ones?"
  - "What about at the sight station?"
  - "What do you think would happen if we didn't have senses?"
- Brainstorm different types of food with the students. Tell the students they are going to use their five senses to describe their favorite foods.

My Five Senses Poem *(cont.)*

- Model for them using your favorite food. For example, a poem for an apple might go like this:

> *I sound very crunchy.*
> *I taste very sweet, but sometimes tangy.*
> *I smell very good.*
> *I feel smooth.*
> *I look round and red.*
> *I am an apple!*

- Have the students fill out the **My Five Senses Poem** planning sheet. They will use this when they go to the computer. Emphasize to students they will have to use their imaginations and creativity, especially for the senses of sound and touch.

On the computer:

- Open the (*Sense.doc*) template from the CD-ROM.
- Delete the red text that says (*type your name here*) and type your name.
- Delete the red text that says (*type your favorite food here*) and type the name of your favorite food.
- Delete the red text that says (*type what your food sounds like*) and type the sound.
- Repeat for the senses of taste, smell, touch, and sight.
- On the last line, delete the red text and type in your favorite food again.

Extensions:

- Allow the students to use a digital camera to take pictures of their favorite foods to include with their poems.
- Let the students bring in samples of their favorite foods and explain their poems to the class.
- Have the students choose their favorite seasons and write poems about what that season sounds like, tastes like, smells like, feels like, and looks like.

My Five Senses Poem

By (type your name here)

My favorite food is (type your favorite food here.).

I sound (type what your food sounds like),

I taste (type what your food tastes like),

I smell (type what your food smells like),

I feel (type what your food feels like),

My Five Senses Poem *(cont.)*

Step-by-Step Instructions

Step 1

Open the (*Sense.doc*) template from the CD-ROM.

Step 2

Select the first line of red text by clicking, holding, and dragging the cursor over the text. Make sure to only select the red text.

By (type your name here)

Step 3

Type your name to replace the red text. As long as you have selected the text, your typed text will replace the red text.

Step 4

Select the next line of red text.

My favorite food is (type your favorite food here.).

Step 5

Now type your favorite food to replace the red text.

Step 6

Repeat steps 4 and 5 for the next five lines of red text, using your planning sheet as a guide for what to type.

Step 7

Select the last line of red text. Now type in your favorite food, which is the same as what you typed for step 5.

Step 8

To save your document, pull down the **FILE** menu and select *Save As*. Give your file the name (*senses your initials*).

Step 9

If you want to print, pull down the **FILE** menu and select *Print*. Click **OK** (PC) or **Print** (Mac).

My Five Senses Poem *(cont.)*

Name _____

Planning Sheet

My favorite food is _____.

I sound _____.

I taste _____.

I smell _____.

I feel _____.

I look _____.

I am _____!

Tangram Fun

A Puzzle Activity

In this project, students will learn how to use the rotate and flip functions of *Microsoft Word*. They will also gain experience with manipulating tangrams.

Grade Levels: 2–3

Materials:

- set of tangram manipulatives
- (*Tangram.doc*) template from the CD-ROM

Before the computer:

- Allow students to practice with physical tangram manipulatives before sending them to the computer to work with the digital versions.
- Students should be taught how to rotate and flip objects in *Microsoft Word* using the **Drawing Toolbar**.

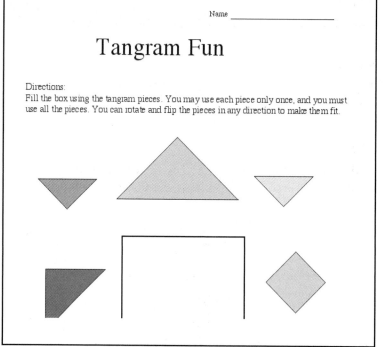

On the computer:

- Open the (*Tangram.doc*) template from the CD-ROM.
- Using the **Drawing Toolbar**, rotate and flip the tangram shapes so that they can fit in the square.
- Make sure students have access to real tangram manipulatives while they work on the computer. You might even want them to have a correctly completed tangram square to look at while creating the one on the computer.

Extensions:

- Allow students to create their own shapes with real tangram pieces, and then duplicate their efforts on the computer.

Internet Resources:

  http://www.geocities.com/TimesSquare/Dungeon/8896/

  http://www.hackersoftware.com/tangrams/

  http://www.geocities.com/TimesSquare/Arcade/1335/

  http://enchantedmind.com/tangram/tangram.htm

  http://www.kidscom.com/orakc/Games/Tangram/tangramright.shtml

Tangram Fun *(cont.)*

Step-by-Step Instructions

Step 1

Open the (*Tangram.doc*) template from the CD-ROM.

Step 2

Type your name at the top right of the page. First click to the right of the word *Name*, and then use the keyboard to type.

Step 3

Make sure you have access to the **Drawing Toolbar**. Pull down the **VIEW** menu and select **Toolbars**. From the toolbars pop-up menu, move over to the right and down to *Drawing*.

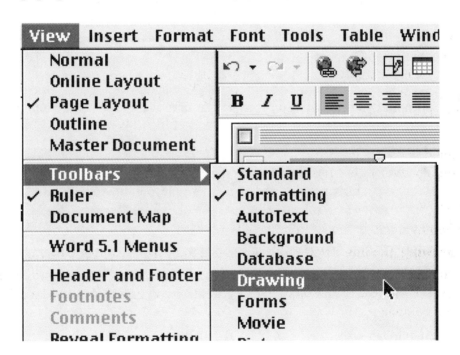

Step 4

Select one of the tangram shapes by clicking on it once. You will notice the little sizing handles around the edges of the tangram shape. Any rotating or flipping you do will apply to this selected shape.

Tangram Fun *(cont.)*

Step 5

With your shape selected, pull down (or up!) the **DRAW** menu from the **Drawing Toolbar** and select *Rotate* or *Flip*. You can choose to **Rotate Left, Rotate Right, Flip Horizontal, Flip Vertical,** or **Free Rotate**.

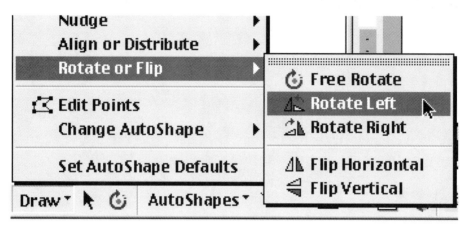

Step 6

After rotating and/or flipping your tangram piece, you can drag it into the square and position it where you want it.

Step 7

Repeat steps 4–6 with the rest of the tangram pieces. Try to place them so they all fit inside the square!

Step 8

When you are done, pull down the **FILE** menu and select *Save As*. Give your file the name (*Tangram your initials*).

Step 9

Pull down the **FILE** menu and select *Print*. Click **OK** (PC) or **Print** (Mac).

Tangram Fun *(cont.)*

Template

Directions: Fill the box using the tangram pieces. You may use each piece only once, and you must use all the pieces. You can rotate and flip the pieces in any direction to make them fit.

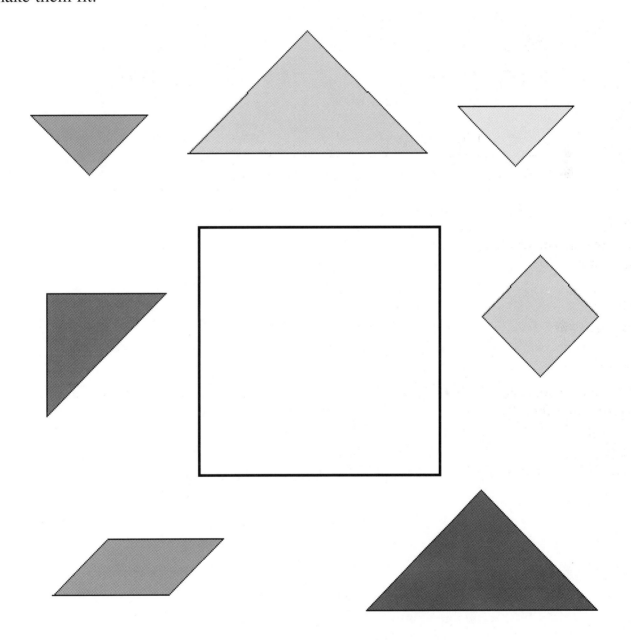

Six Tangram Squares

A Puzzle Activity

In this project, students will extend their knowledge of the rotating capabilities in *Microsoft Word* by using the **Free Rotate** menu option. They will also be challenged by an intriguing task involving several tangram puzzles!

Grade Levels: 2–3

Materials:

- set of tangram manipulatives
- (*6Tangram.doc*) template from the CD-ROM

Before the computer:

- Allow students to practice with physical tangram manipulatives before sending them to the computer to work with the digital versions. Provide them with the six different-sized squares for use with the tangrams.
- Students should be taught how to free rotate objects in *Microsoft Word* using the **Drawing Toolbar**.

On the computer:

- Open the (*6Tangram.doc*) template from the CD-ROM.
- Using the **Drawing Toolbar**, rotate and flip the tangram shapes so they can fit in the squares. You will need more than one of each tangram shape. Copy and paste the shapes as needed.
- Make sure you bring real tangram manipulatives for students to use while you work on the computer. This is a very difficult puzzle, and having the real pieces to look at will help a lot!

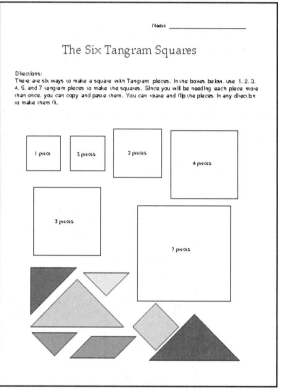

Extensions:

- Once students have been successful in completing this challenge, have them write step-by-step directions on how they did it, including the rotating and flipping of the tangram shapes.

Internet Resources:

> **http://www.geocities.com/TimesSquare/Dungeon/8896/**
> **http://www.hackersoftware.com/tangrams/**
> **http://www.geocities.com/TimesSquare/Arcade/1335/**
> **http://enchantedmind.com/tangram/tangram.htm**
> **http://www.kidscom.com/orakc/Games/Tangram/tangramright.shtml**

Six Tangram Squares *(cont.)*

Step-by-Step Instructions

Step 1

Open the (*6Tangram.doc*) template from the CD-ROM.

Step 2

Type your name at the top right of the page. First click to the right of the word *Name*, and then use the keyboard to type.

Step 3

Make sure you have access to the **Drawing Toolbar**. Pull down the **VIEW** menu and select *Toolbars*. From the toolbars pop-up menu, move over to the right and down to *Drawing*.

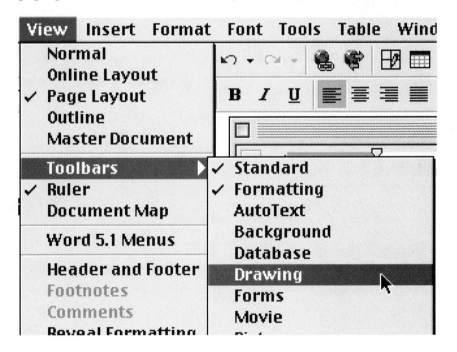

Step 4

Select one of the tangram shapes by clicking on it once. You will notice the little sizing handles around the edges of the tangram shape. Any rotating or flipping you do will apply to this selected shape.

Six Tangram Squares *(cont.)*

Step 5

With your shape selected, pull down (or up!) the **DRAW** menu from the **Drawing Toolbar** and select *Rotate* or *Flip*. You can choose to **Rotate Left**, **Rotate Right**, **Flip Horizontal**, **Flip Vertical**, or **Free Rotate**.

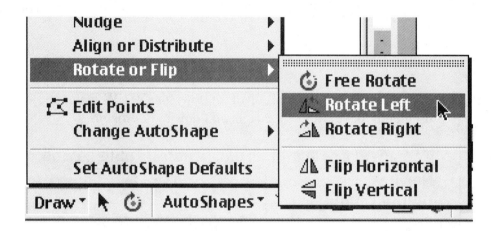

Step 6

After rotating and/or flipping your tangram piece, you can drag it into the square and position it where you want. Make sure to pay attention to how many pieces to use in each square!

Step 7

Since you will need more than one copy of each of the pieces, you can copy and paste them to create additional ones. To do this, click once on a tangram piece to select it. Go to the **FILE** menu and select *Copy*. Then go to the **FILE** menu again and select *Paste*. You will have another copy of the piece!

Step 8

Repeat steps 4–6 with the rest of the tangram pieces. Try to place them so they all fit inside the squares.

Step 9

When you are done, pull down the **FILE** menu and select *Save As*. Give your file the name (*6 Tangram Squares your initials*).

Step 10

Pull down the **FILE** menu and select *Print*. Click **OK** (PC) or **Print** (Mac).

Six Tangram Squares *(cont.)*

Example Page

Directions: There are six ways to make a square with tangram pieces. In the boxes below, use 1, 2, 3, 4, 5, 6, and 7 tangram pieces to make the squares. Since you need each piece more than once, you can copy and paste them. You can rotate and flip the pieces in any direction to make them fit.

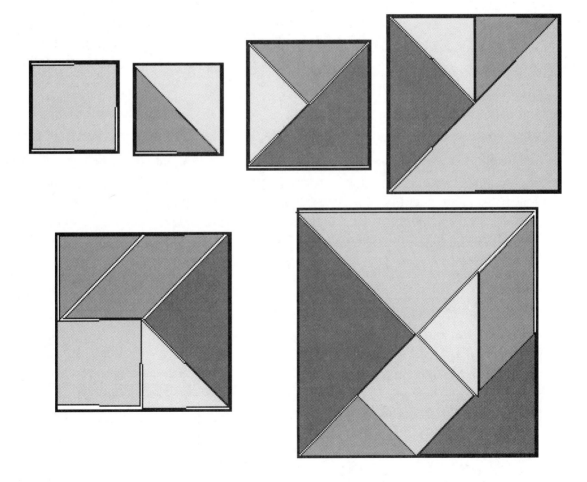

Tic-Tac-Toe

A Game of Strategy

This project is a good way to introduce your students to the use of the **Line** and **Oval** tools. By playing a game with which they are familiar, they will gain a better understanding of how these tools are used. This is also a good lesson to use to teach your students how to cooperate and take turns at the computer.

Grade Levels: K–3

Materials:

- pencil and paper, or a tic-tac-toe game
- (*Tictac.doc*) template from the CD-ROM

Before the computer:

- Allow the students to play tic-tac-toe away from the computer using either pencil and paper or a tic-tac-toe game.
- As they are playing, ask questions to get them thinking about strategies:
  - "If you have the first turn, where would you start? Why?"
  - "Does it matter if you are 0 or X?"
  - "Is it better to have the first turn? Why?"
  - "What kinds of strategies do you use?"
  - "Are there any tricks you use to try to fool your partner? What are they?"
- This game requires two players. Start as a whole-class lesson with two volunteer students at the computer. Have them model good partner behavior at the computer (taking turns, being a good winner, strategies for helping partner with any problems, etc.). Get feedback from the class and have them generate a list of good partner behaviors as you write them on chart paper. Post this list at the computer.

On the computer:

- Open the (*Tictac.doc*) template from the CD-ROM.
- Take turns with your partner using the **Line** and **Oval** tools to make X's and 0's.
- The first player to get three in a row wins.
- To play another game, you can use the **Delete** or **Backspace** key on the keyboard to delete the X's and 0's.

Extensions:

- Allow the students to play a 4 x 4 matrix of the game. They can play first on paper, then design the template on the computer in *Microsoft Word*.
- A variation of the 4 x 4 matrix is to allow three or four in a row to be a winner.
- Have students write about their strategies for winning the game.

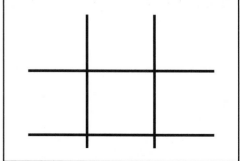

Tic-Tac-Toe

Use the line tool and the oval tool to play tic-tac-toe. When you are done with your first game, use the delete or backspace key to delete your X's and 0's and play again!

Tic-Tac-Toe *(cont.)*

Step-by-Step Instructions

Step 1

Open the (*Tictac.doc*) template from the CD-ROM.

Step 2

Make sure you have access to the **Drawing Toolbar**. Pull down the **VIEW** menu and select *Toolbars*. From the toolbars pop-up menu, move over to the right and down to *Drawing*.

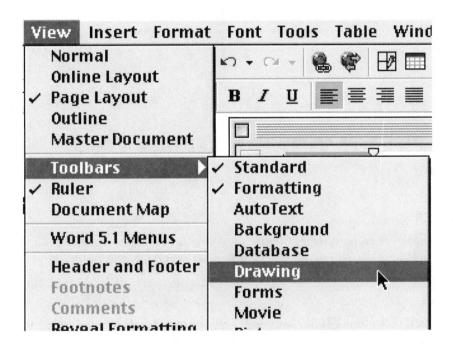

Step 3

Player one takes his or her turn. From the **Drawing Toolbar** use the **Oval** tool for the 0's and the Line tool for X's.

Step 4

Click on the proper tool, and move your mouse to the square where you wish to make your first mark.

Tic-Tac-Toe *(cont.)*

Step 5

Click, hold, and drag the mouse to create your oval. If you are making an X, you will have to use the **Line** tool twice, once for each part of the X.

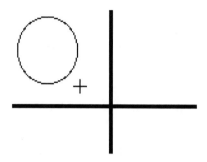

Step 6

If your X or 0 is not exactly where you want it, you can move it by clicking, holding, and dragging it to the new location.

Step 7

When you are finished with the game, you can save and print if you like (see steps 8 and 9). If you are done, pull down the **FILE** menu and select *Quit*. If you want to play another game, you can delete the X's and 0's by clicking on them and using the **Delete** or **Backspace** key on the keyboard.

Step 8

To save your game, pull down the **FILE** menu and select *Save As*. Give your file the name (*tictactoe your initials*).

Step 9

If you want to print, pull down the **FILE** menu and select *Print*. Click **OK** (PC) or **Print** (Mac). Make sure to print two copies, one for you and one for your partner!

Tic-Tac-Toe *(cont.)*

Example Page

Directions: Use the **Line** tool and the **Oval** tool to play tic-tac-toe. When you are done with your first game, use the **Delete** or **Backspace** key to delete your X's and O's, and play again!

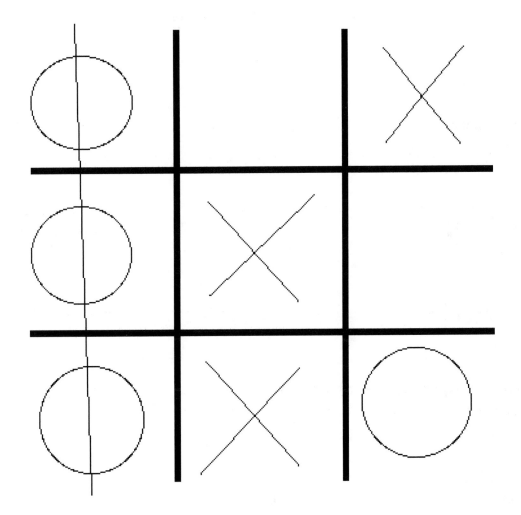

Coins All aRound Us!

Investigating Money

In this project, students will practice using the drawing tools, specifically the **Line** tool, to match coins with their values. They will reinforce their understanding of the value of the penny, nickel, dime, and quarter.

Grade Levels: K–2

Materials:

- coins (either play or real)
- (*Coin.doc*) template from the CD-ROM

Before the computer:

- Review with the students the four coins. Allow them some hands-on time to play and investigate. This activity would be a good addition to your existing lessons on money.
- Get them thinking by asking questions such as:
  - "What shapes are the coins?"
  - "What colors are they?"
  - "Are they the same size?"
  - "Are the bigger ones always worth more?"
  - "If you could have 10 of any of the coins, which would you rather have? Why?"
  - "What could you buy with four of the biggest coins? With four of the copper ones?"

On the computer:

- Open the (*Coin.doc*) template from the CD-ROM.
- Use the **Line** tool to match the pictures of the coins with their values.

Extensions:

- Have students copy and paste the coins to make sums of money (i.e., How many ways can you make 23 cents?).

Coins All aRound Us!

Use the line tool to draw a line from the coins on the left to their values on the right.

25 cents

5 cents

Partial image of *Coin.doc*

Coins All aRound Us! *(cont.)*

Step-by-Step Instructions

Step 1

Open the (*Coin.doc*) template from the CD-ROM.

Step 2

Make sure you have access to the **Drawing Toolbar**. Pull down the **VIEW** menu and select *Toolbars*. From the toolbars pop-up menu, move over to the right and down to *Drawing*.

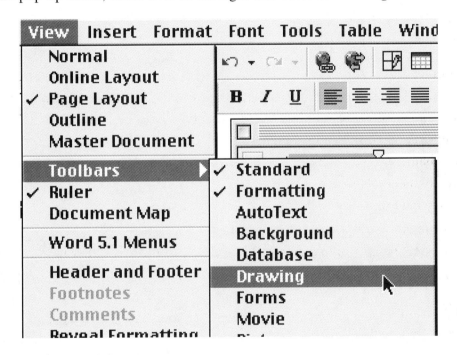

Step 3

Select the **Line** tool by clicking on it.

Coins All aRound Us! *(cont.)*

Step 4

Move your cursor next to one of the coins, and click and hold the mouse. Draw a line by dragging the mouse to the correct value for that coin on the right side of the page.

25 cents

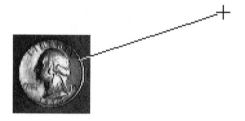

5 cents

Step 5

Repeat step 4 for each of the coins. If you make a mistake, you can click on a line and use the **Delete** or **Backspace** key on the keyboard to delete it.

Step 6

See if you can figure out how to put an arrow at the end of your line! (Hint: Look at the **Drawing Toolbar** next to the **Line** tool.)

Step 7

When you are done, pull down the **FILE** menu and select *Save As*. Give your file the name (*coins your initials*).

Step 8

Pull down the **FILE** menu and select *Print*. Click **OK** (PC) or **Print** (Mac).

Coins All aRound Us! *(cont.)*

Example Page

Directions: Use the **Line** tool to draw a line from the coins on the left to their values on the right.

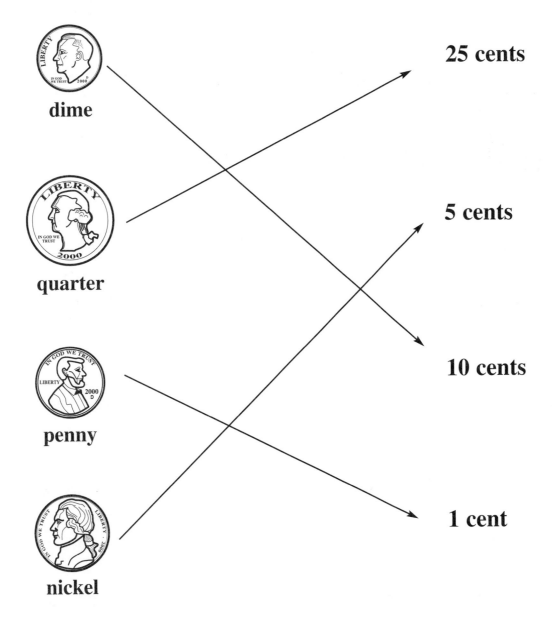

Shapes, Colors, and Lines

If you are teaching your students about shapes and colors, this activity will give your students an opportunity to reinforce their knowledge while gaining experience with the **AutoShapes**, **Line**, **Rectangle**, **Oval**, **Fill Color**, and **Line Color** tools in *Microsoft Word*. Students will be prompted to create various shapes in different colors as they explore these tools.

Grade Levels: K–2

Materials:

- (*Shapes.doc*) template from CD-ROM
- a printed copy of the template for the students to use as a planning sheet (page 77)

Before the computer:

- Print out a copy of the blank template to use as a planning sheet (or use page 77).
- To help the students review and recognize shapes, see what objects they can find around the classroom that are certain shapes—circles, ovals, squares, rectangles, triangles, and lines.
- Allow them to complete the printout of the template at their desks before going to the computer. You might want to do this as a whole-group lesson.
- Make sure you demonstrate the tools on the **Drawing Toolbar** before allowing the students to start on the computer. On the template, each shape to be drawn is designated two ways: with words and with a small drawing to assist your nonreaders.
- You might ask them a few questions to get them thinking:
  - "Can you make a square with more than one tool?"
  - "How do you think you could make a perfect circle with the oval tool?"
  - "How many ways do you think you could make a triangle?"

On the computer:

- Open the (*Shapes.doc*) template from the CD-ROM.
- Use the **Drawing Tools** to make the shapes.
- Use the **Fill Color** tool to color in your shapes.
- See if you can make the shapes using more than one tool. For example, can you make a triangle using the **Line** tool?

Extensions:

- If your students think of shapes that are not on the template, allow them to create those with the **Drawing Tools** as well.
- If any students come up with novel ways of making shapes, make sure to let them share their techniques with the rest of the class.

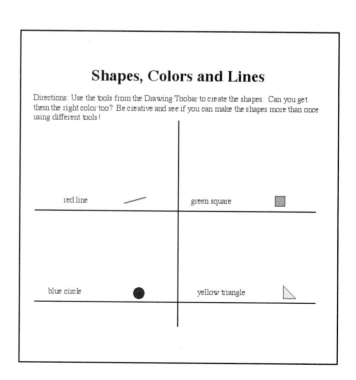

Shapes, Colors and Lines

Directions: Use the tools from the Drawing Toolbar to create the shapes. Can you get them the right color too? Be creative and see if you can make the shapes more than once using different tools!

| red line | | green square | |
| blue circle | | yellow triangle | |

Shapes, Colors, and Lines *(cont.)*

Step-by-Step Instructions

Step 1

Open the (*Shapes.doc*) template from the CD-ROM.

Step 2

Make sure you have access to the **Drawing Toolbar**. Pull down the **VIEW** menu and select *Toolbars*. From the toolbars pop-up menu, move over to the right and down to *Drawing*.

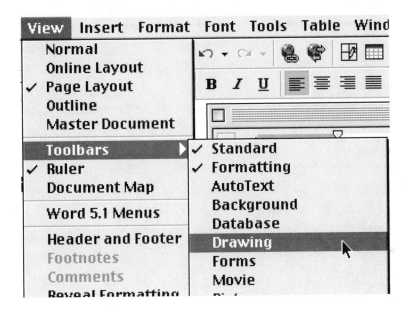

Step 3

The first shape we get to draw is a red line. Start by clicking on the **Line** tool.

Step 4

Move your mouse to where you want to make your line. Your cursor will be a crosshair. Now click, hold and drag to draw your line.

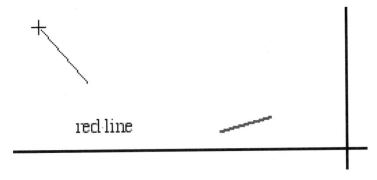

Shapes, Colors, and Lines *(cont.)*

Step 5

Now we need to make the line red. Click once on the line so it is selected. You know it is selected if it has the two little handles on it, one on each end.

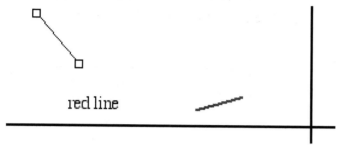

Step 6

Use the **Line Color** tool to choose the color for the line. Since the line was selected when you chose the color, the color will only apply to the line.

Step 7

Your line should now be red! The next shape is a green square. Use the **Rectangle** tool to make the square. Can you figure out how to make a perfect square instead of a rectangle?

Step 8

Use the **Fill** tool to color in your square. Don't forget to select your square first!

Step 9

Continue to draw the shapes. Remember, for some of them, you will need to use the **AutoShapes Tools**.

Step 10

To save your game, pull down the **FILE** menu and select *Save As*. Give your file the name (*shapes your initials*).

Step 11

If you want to print, pull down the **FILE** menu and select *Print*. Click **OK** (PC) or **Print** (Mac).

Shapes, Colors, and Lines *(cont.)*

Example Page/Planning Sheet

Directions: Use the tools from the **Drawing Toolbar** to create the shapes. Can you get them the right color too? Be creative and see if you can make the shapes more than once using different tools!

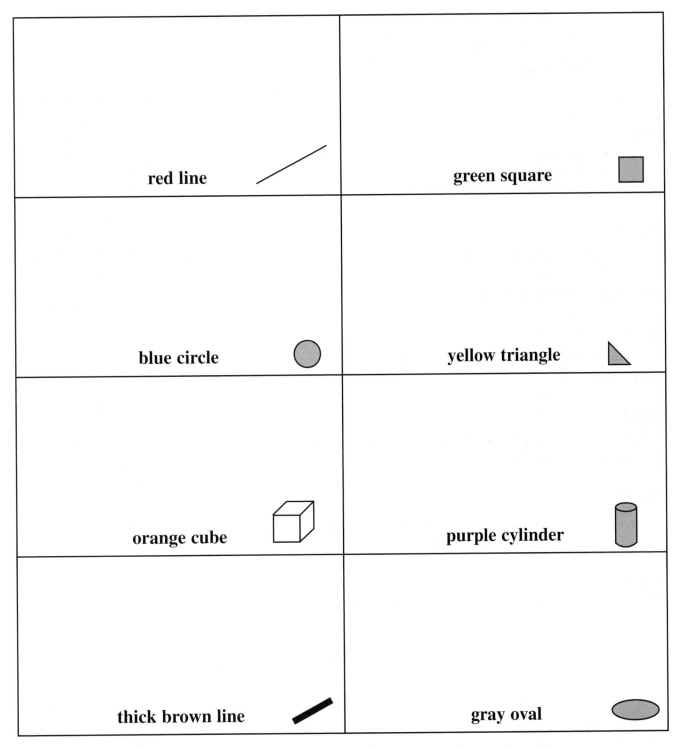

red line	green square
blue circle	yellow triangle
orange cube	purple cylinder
thick brown line	gray oval

How Could We Get There?

In this project, students will identify different types of transportation that can be used to get to various destinations. While completing the project, they will gain experience with dragging objects and creating text boxes in *Microsoft Word.*

Grade Levels: K–2

Materials:

- (*There.doc*) template from the CD-ROM
- a brainstormed list of places to which students can walk or drive

Before the computer:

- If you haven't talked about Venn diagrams with your students, introduce them here. You may want to practice by completing a class Venn diagram on a subject of common interest.
- Discuss with the students about walking and driving. Stimulate conversation with questions such as:
    - "Why do we have cars? Why can't we just walk everywhere?"
    - "Tell me some places you have walked to before. Why didn't you drive?"
    - "Tell me some other places where you have gone in a car. Why didn't you walk?"
    - "Is walking or driving better? Why?"
    - "Are there some places you could walk and drive? Why would you walk there sometimes, and other times go in a car?"
    - "Which is your favorite, walking or driving? Why?"
- Brainstorm with the students places where they could walk to or drive.

On the computer:

- Open the (*There.doc*) template from the CD-ROM.
- Drag the words of the places to go into the proper places on the Venn diagram.
- Create your own text boxes and type in places you can think of where you could walk or drive.

Extensions:

- Change the modes of transportation from drive/walk to fly/boat.
- Allow the students to import clip art or photographs to depict the locations.

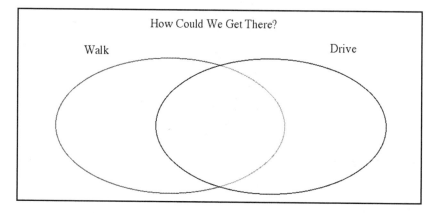

How Could We Get There? *(cont.)*

Step-by-Step Instructions

Step 1
Open the (*There.doc*) template from the CD-ROM.

Step 2
Click once on a word to highlight the text box. The text box will have a shaded border surrounding it after you click on it.

Step 3
Move the cursor so it is on the shaded edge of the text box. The cursor will change into a double arrow.

Step 4
Click, hold, and drag the text box into the correct place on the Venn diagram.

Step 5
Repeat for the remaining text boxes, dragging each one to the correct place on the Venn diagram.

Step 6
Now let's create a few text boxes with words you type. Go to the **INSERT** menu and choose *Text Box*.

Step 7
Move your cursor into your document, and you will see it has changed into a cross.

How Could We Get There? *(cont.)*

Step 8

Click, hold, and drag your cursor to create a rectangle. This is your text box.

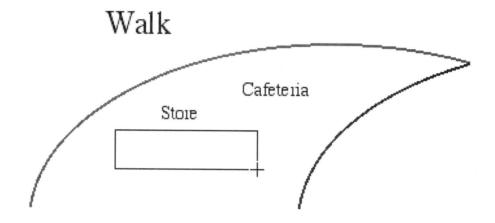

Step 9

Using the keyboard, type a place to which you could walk, drive, or walk and drive.

Step 10

Repeat steps 2 through 4 to move your newly created text box to the Venn diagram.

Step 11

To save your document, pull down the **FILE** menu and select *Save A*s. Give your file the name (*walkdrive your initials*).

Step 12

If you want to print, pull down the **FILE** menu and select ***Print***. Click **OK** (PC) or **Print** (Mac).

How Could We Get There? *(cont.)*

Example Page

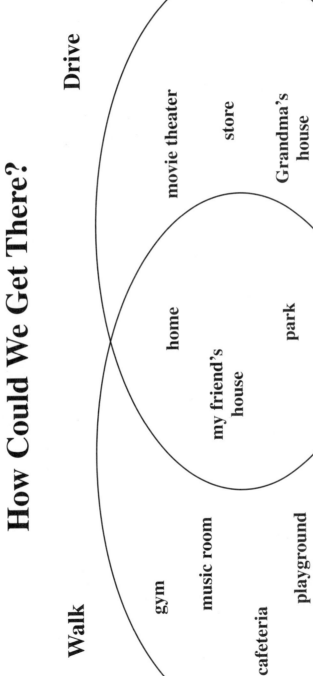

Drive

movie theater

store

Grandma's house

home

my friend's house

park

gym

music room

cafeteria

playground

Walk

How Could We Get There?

The Important Thing About School

After reading *The Important Book* by Margaret Wise Brown, the students will write about important things about their school. They will gain experience with selecting text and keyboarding in *Microsoft Word*.

Grade Levels: 1–3

Materials:

- (*Thing.doc*) template from the CD-ROM
- copies of **The Important Thing About School** planning sheet–page 84 (also available on the CD-ROM as *Thingpl.doc*)
- a brainstormed list of important things about your school
- *The Important Book* by Margaret Wise Brown

Before the computer:

- Read *The Important Book* by Margaret Wise Brown to your students.
- Brainstorm with the students things they think are important about their school. Get them thinking with questions such as:
  - "What makes something important?"
  - "What do you think is important about school in general?"
  - "What is important about your school?"
- Have the students fill out **The Important Thing About School** planning sheet to take to the computer with them (page 84).

On the computer:

- Open the (*Thing.doc*) template from the CD-ROM.
- Begin with the most important thing about school to you. Type this on the first line.
- Think of other things that are important to you about school. Type in five other things that are important about school.
- On the last line, type in the most important thing about school again.

Extensions:

- Take pictures of important things around your school and allow the students to insert pictures of the important things into their *Microsoft Word* documents.
- Have the students write why they think these things are important about school.
- Let the students come up with different topics in addition to school and complete the activity with their new ideas. Your students will love to write about their pets, their families, and even their teacher in this familiar prose!

> ### The Important Thing About School
>
> The important thing about school is (type the most important thing about school here.).
>
> It (type another important thing about school here),
>
> and (type another important thing about school),

The Important Thing About School *(cont.)*

Step-by-Step Instructions

Step 1

Open the (*Thing.doc*) template from the CD-ROM.

Step 2

Select the first line of red text by clicking, holding, and dragging the cursor over the text. Make sure to select only the red text.

The important thing about school is (type the most important thing about school here.).

Step 3

Using your planning sheet as a guide, type the most important thing about school. As long as you have selected the text, your typed text will replace the red text.

Step 4

Select the next line of red text.

Step 5

Now type the next important thing about school.

Step 6

Repeat steps 4 and 5 for the next four lines of red text, typing in a different important thing about school each time.

Step 7

Select the last line of red text. Now type in the most important thing about school, which is the same as what you typed for step 3.

Step 8

To save your document, pull down the **FILE** menu and select *Save As*. Give your file the name (*important your initials*).

Step 9

If you want to print, pull down the **FILE** menu and select *Print*. Click **OK** (PC) or **Print** (Mac).

The Important Thing About School *(cont.)*

Name _____

Planning Sheet

The important thing about school is _____

_____.

It_____,

and _____,

and _____,

and _____,

and _____.

But the important thing about school is _____

_____.

State Trading Cards

In this project, the students will conduct research on the state in which they live and create state trading cards. They will be introduced to the WordArt capability of *Microsoft Word* as they fill in their State Trading Card templates.

Grade Levels: 2–3

Materials:

- (*State.doc*) template from the CD-ROM
- nonfiction resources on your state
- copies of the **State Trading Card** planning sheet–page 88 (also available on the CD-ROM as *Statepl.doc*)
- Internet resources:

  http://www.ipl.org/youth/stateknow/skhome.html
  http://www.americaslibrary.gov/cgi-bin/page.cgi/es

Before the computer:

- Expose the students to nonfiction materials about their states during social studies or silent reading time. If you have trouble locating materials on your state, visit the Web sites listed above and print some information.
- If you have the capability of projecting your computer to a TV screen or computer projector, visit some of the Web sites listed above with your students.
- Have your students fill out the **State Trading Cards** planning sheet before going to the computer. You might want to have your students work in pairs.

On the computer:

- Open the (*State.doc*) template from the CD-ROM.
- Type in the name of your state using the **Edit WordArt Text** dialog box.
- Delete the red text that says (*type your state bird here*) and type the name of the state bird.
- Delete the red text that says (*type your state flower here*) and type the name of the flower.
- Delete the red text that says (*type your state capital here*) and type the city name.
- After printing, use the box at the bottom to draw a symbol that represents your state.

Extensions:

- On the back of the card, have each student write a favorite thing about his/her state and why it is his/her favorite.
- Allow students to do further research on their states and share their findings with classmates.
- Have students conduct research on other states, and compile many state cards for the class library.
- Let the students come up with different topics in addition to states for creating trading cards.

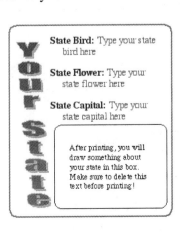

State Trading Cards *(cont.)*

Step-by-Step Instructions

Step 1

Open the (*State.doc*) template from the CD-ROM.

Step 2

Click on the *Your State* text to highlight the text box (you may have to click on it twice). This is a special type of text box called WordArt.

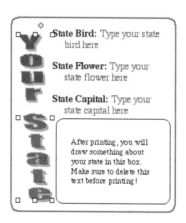

Step 3

The **WordArt Toolbar** comes up. Click on **Edit Text**.

Step 4

Type in the name of your state in the box.

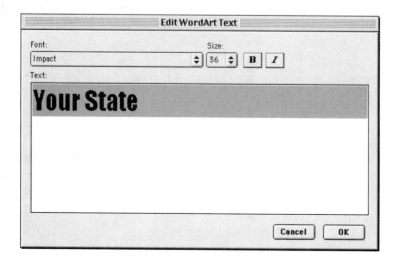

State Trading Cards *(cont.)*

Step 5

Select the red text after the words *State Bird* and type the name of your state bird.

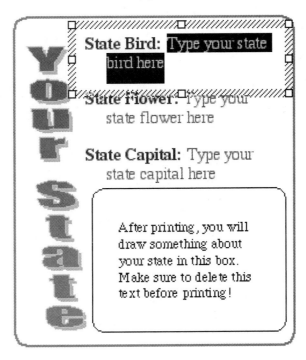

Step 6

Repeat step 5 for the *State Flower* and the *State Capital*.

Step 7

Delete the text in the box at the bottom of the card. You can click the mouse at the end of the text and use the **Backspace** or **Delete** key.

Step 8

To save your document, pull down the **FILE** menu and select *Save As*. Give your file the name (*mystate your initials*).

Step 9

To print, pull down the **FILE** menu and select *Print*. Click **OK** (PC) or **Print** (Mac).

Step 10

After printing, use colored pencils or markers to draw something that represents your state in the box at the bottom of your trading card. Possible choices might include your state flag, state bird, an outline of your state, or the state flower. Use your imagination!

State Trading Cards *(cont.)*

Name _____

Planning Sheet

The name of my state is

_____

My state bird is

_____

My state flower is

_____

My state capital is

_____

Picture that represents the state

Create Your Own *Word* Search!

How can you get students excited and motivated to learn and become familiar with new vocabulary? Let them create their own activity pages, that's how! In this project, students create their own word search puzzles related to your current theme in social studies. Your students will search for new and challenging vocabulary words as they create their word searches, and then challenge their classmates to complete the puzzles. They will gain experience working with tables in *Microsoft Word* as they complete this activity.

Grade Levels: 1–3

Materials:

- (*Search.doc*) template from the CD-ROM
- a printed copy of the Word Search template for students to use as a planning sheet (page 92)
- a teacher- or student-generated list of social studies vocabulary

Before the computer:

- Explain to the students that they will be creating word searches for their classmates to solve.
- Supply the students with a vocabulary list of current social studies words, and/or allow them to generate their own from resources you are using for social studies (textbooks, trade books, Internet sites, etc.).
- Give them a word search to solve, then ask them some questions such as:
  - "What did you like best about the word search? Why?"
  - "Were some of the words harder to find than others? What made them harder?"
  - "What kinds of things do you have to be thinking about if two words in your word search intersect?"
  - "When you make your own word search, what could you do to make it more challenging to find the words?"
- You might want to allow your students to create a word search on paper before coming to the computer. If so, print out the template from the CD-ROM for them to use as a planning sheet.

On the computer:

- Open the (*Search.doc*) template from the CD-ROM.
- Type your vocabulary words in the word box at the bottom of the template.
- Next type your words in the word search. You can type them horizontally, vertically, or diagonally. For an extra challenge, try backwards!
- After typing in all of your words in the word search, fill in the blank squares with random letters of your choice.

Extensions:

- The students will be eager to create word searches for subjects other than social studies. Let them come up with ideas for additional word search topics.
- Challenge your more advanced students with the task of creating a crossword puzzle. They could start with the word search template or create their own.

Create Your Own *Word* Search! *(cont.)*

Step-by-Step Instructions

Step 1

Open the (*Search.doc*) template from the CD-ROM.

Step 2

Scroll down to the word box at the bottom of the page.

Step 3

Move the cursor and click to the right of the number one. Type your first vocabulary word.

Word Box

1.	7.
2.	8.
3.	9.
4.	10.
5.	11.
6.	12.

Step 4

Repeat step 3 with your next vocabulary word, and type it next to number 2.

Step 5

Repeat for the remainder of your vocabulary words. Don't forget to capitalize proper nouns!

Step 6

Scroll to the top of your word search. Choose the square where you would like to begin your first vocabulary word.

Step 7

Click once with the mouse in the square. You will either see the blinking insertion point, or the square will be highlighted.

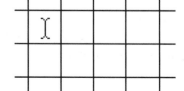

Step 8

Type your letter from the keyboard. Repeat step 7 for each of the letters in your word.

Create Your Own *Word* Search! *(cont.)*

Step 9

Decide where your second word will go. If it has any of the same letters as your first word, you might be able to intersect the two words.

Step 10

Repeat steps 7 and 8 to complete your second word.

Step 11

Continue until you have typed all your words into the word search.

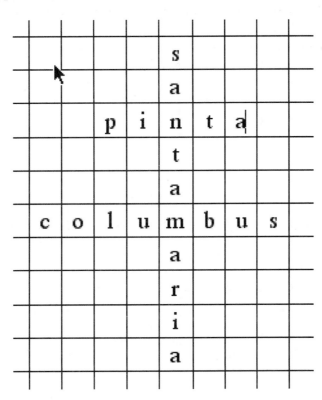

Step 12

Fill in all of the empty squares with random letters. Can you think of any ways to make the word search more difficult to solve while completing this last step?

Step 13

To save your document, pull down the **FILE** menu and select *Save As*. Give your file the name (*wordsearch your initials*).

Step 14

If you want to print, pull down the **FILE** menu and select *Print*. Click **OK** (PC) or **Print** (Mac).

Create Your Own *Word* Search! *(cont.)*

Name _____

Planning Sheet/Template

Directions: Type your words into the word search horizontally, vertically, and diagonally. After you type in all of your words, fill in the empty spaces with random letters. Make sure to type your words into the word box, too. Print your puzzle and see if your friends can find all of your words!

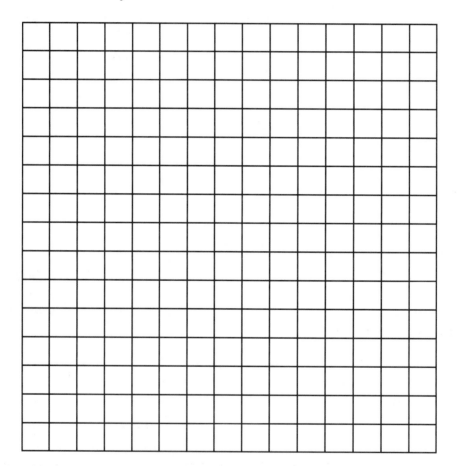

Word Box	
1.	7.
2.	8.
3.	9.
4.	10.
5.	11.
6.	12.

Microsoft Word: Tips and Tricks

There are many useful, fun, and interesting things you can do with *Microsoft Word*. What follows are a few tips and tricks to help get you started with some of the features of *Microsoft Word*. Don't forget about the **HELP** menu! From the **HELP** menu, you can pull down to *Microsoft Word Help* to type in a question or *Contents and Index* to get a list of general help topics or all topics in alphabetical order.

Wizards and Templates

There are built-in functions in *Microsoft Word* that have started the job for you! A template is a pre-existing form that you open and customize to your specific needs. The documents the students are using from the CD-ROM are templates. A wizard asks you a series of questions and then uses your responses to help you prepare the document. To access the built-in templates and wizards in *Microsoft Word*, pull down the **FILE** menu and select **New**. Explore the tabs at the top of the window. You can tell the difference between a wizard and a template by its name and its icon in this window. The wizards have a little magic wand over the icon and end in the word wizard.

Elegant Letter

Letter Wizard

You can download additional templates and clip art from the Microsoft Web site at:

http://cgl.microsoft.com/clipgallerylive/

Working with Color in *Microsoft Word*

There are many ways to apply and work with color in *Microsoft Word*. You can apply color to text or objects. With objects, you can usually specify the line color (border) and the fill color (inside). Color options can be accessed from the **Drawing Toolbar**, the **FORMAT** menu (pull down to *Font*, *Object*, or *Picture*) or the **Format Toolbar**.

If you want to apply color to a drawing object, first click on it once to select it. Then go to the **Drawing Toolbar** and click on the **Fill Color** or **Line Color** tools. You can also click on the **Line Style** tool to change the thickness of the line or the border of an object.

To apply color changes to text, first select the text by clicking, holding, and dragging across it. Now use the **Font Color** tool in the **Drawing Toolbar** or the **Formatting Toolbar** to select a different color for your text. You can also click on the **FORMAT** menu, pull down to *Font*, and use the **Color** option in the dialog box.

Tables in *Microsoft Word*

Were you wondering how the template for the word search was made? This template incorporated the use of Tables, which gives you great flexibility for formatting elements in your document. To insert a table in your document, you can click on the **INSERT** menu and pull down to *Table*, or you can use the **Insert Table** button from the toolbar. After you create a table, the **Tables and Borders** button gives you several options for changing the appearance of your table.

Microsoft Word: Tips and Tricks *(cont.)*

Word Wrapping

Are you wondering how the text is "wrapped" around the graphics and other pictures in this book? It is quite easy to do in *Microsoft Word*! After selecting the object, shape, or picture, click on the **FORMAT** menu and pull down to the last item. It will say *Picture*, *AutoShape*, or *Object*, depending on what you have selected. You will get the **Format** dialog box. Click on the **Wrapping** tab at the top, and from there you can choose the **Wrapping style** and where you would like the text to be placed relative to the object.

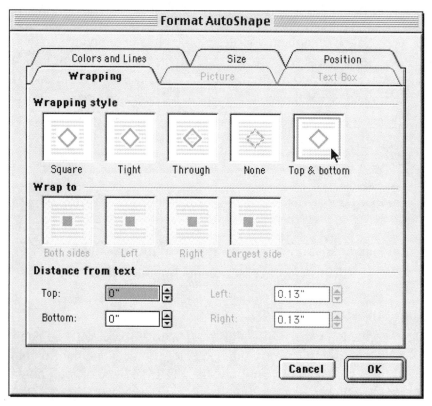

Inserting Simple Shapes

In *Microsoft Word*, you are only two clicks of the mouse from inserting simple shapes into your document. Using the **Drawing Toolbar**, click on the **AutoShapes** button. From here, you can choose from lines, basic shapes, etc. Try it and find out all of the other possibilities! After selecting the shape you want, move your mouse back into your document. Your mouse pointer is now a crosshair. Just click, hold, and drag it to where you want your shape to be, and *voila*!

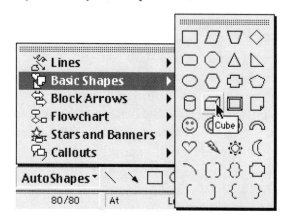

Microsoft Word: Tips and Tricks *(cont.)*

Inserting Fun and Unusual Symbols

Ever wonder how to get a ®, or a π, or even a ✳ in your document? You are just a menu away! Click on the **INSERT** menu and pull down to *Symbol*. From the resulting dialog box, you have many symbols from which to choose. You can even change the set of symbols by changing the font from the pulldown menu.

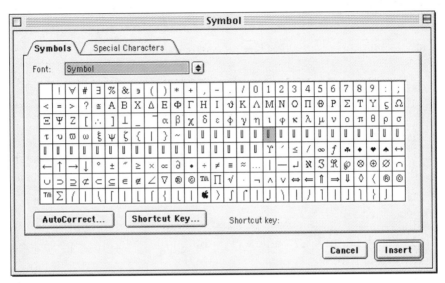

Adding a Picture

Using Clip Art

Microsoft Word has built-in clip art, called the **Microsoft Clip Gallery**. You access these collections by clicking on the **INSERT** menu, pulling down to *Picture*, and then over to *Clip Art*. If you are trying to use clip art from another source (maybe a clip art CD-ROM or a clip art collection from another program) you would use the **INSERT** menu, pull down to *Picture*, and over to *From File* instead of *Clip Art*. You would then locate the file from your hard drive or CD-ROM.

Using Pictures from Scanners, Digital Cameras, and Other Outside Sources

If the Clip Gallery does not satisfy your desire for pictures, you can insert pictures from almost any other source—*Microsoft Word* will read all popular graphic formats. To insert a picture from an outside source, click on the **INSERT** menu, pull down to *Picture*, and over to *From File*. Now, select the picture file from the appropriate folder or directory on your hard drive.

Capturing Pictures from the Internet

The Internet is a wonderful place for students to obtain graphics to use in *Microsoft Word* projects. It is a simple process to copy pictures from Web pages. With both your browser program (*Netscape, Internet Explorer,* etc.) and *Microsoft Word* open, click and hold (Mac) or right-click (PC) on the picture you want on the Web page. From the menu that pops up, choose *Copy Image*. Then switch to your *Word* document, click where you want to place the picture, and select *Paste* from the **EDIT** menu.

Don't forget to use the feature of creating your own clip art galleries in *Word* (see page 11). This is a wonderful way to organize all the pictures from your digital camera, the graphics you have captured from the Internet, etc.

Microsoft Word: Tips and Tricks *(cont.)*

Working with Graphics

Do you want to resize that picture you imported or the AutoShape you have drawn? What about cropping? Would you like to move it to a different part of the page? All is easy to accomplish in *Microsoft Word*. Before you can do any of these things with a graphic, you must first select it. When you click on a graphic, it gets those little handles on its corners and edges. These little handles will do different things with your graphic. If all you want to do is move your graphic, you merely click anywhere on the graphic (not on one of the handles) and drag it to a different place in your document.

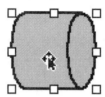

If you want to resize it, you would use one of the handles on the graphic. The corner handles will change the height and width at the same time, while the handles on the edges will change only the width or the height.

To crop a graphic, first make sure you have it selected. Then click on the **Crop** tool (from the **Picture Toolbar**). Move the mouse back to your picture and click, hold, and drag one of the handles. You can use different handles to crop different parts of the graphic.

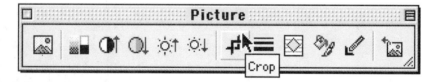

Allowing students to import pictures into their documents will heighten student interest and ownership in their work. This is especially true when the pictures are coming from the students' personal experience—for example, the pictures they took of the animals during their field trip to the zoo!